VISHAL GEORGE

Money Mindsets

Science–Based Stories to Rewire your Money Beliefs, Goals & Habits

First published by Behavioural by Design 2023

First edition

ISBN: 978-1-7385998-0-6

This book was professionally typeset on Reedsy. Find out more at reedsy.com

To my whānau.
Dear family, I am forever in your debt.

&

To Rita.
Thank you for trusting me, opening my heart and sharing your
story with me.

Contents

Acknowledgement   iii
Introduction: My first relationship with money   v

I   Stories of Rita

Rita rewrites her money story   3
Mindset 1. We are wired for curiosity   4
Mindset 2. Framing your own money story   14
Mindset 3. Nudge the system!   24

II   Stories of Rodri

Rodri reroutes his money compass   35
Mindset 4. Power of visualisation   37
Mindset 5. Setting goals with intention   46
Mindset 6. Counting what matters   56

III   Stories of Kaya

Kaya resets her money thermostat   67
Mindset 7. Context creates the habit   69
Mindset 8. Consistency compounds   79
Mindset 9. Reward the small wins   88

Epilogue   96
Bonus Quiz   98
Notes   100
About the Author   106

Acknowledgement

First, I would like to acknowledge *tangata whenua* (people of the land) on which this book was written and published. Recognising Māori guardianship of our beautiful natural environment in *Te Whanganui a Tara* (Wellington), Aotearoa New Zealand, I pay my tribute to *Muaūpoko*, *Ngāti Toa Rangatira*, *Taranaki Whānui ki te Upoko o te Ika* and *Te Atiawa*.

In writing this book, I am merely a vessel for the pioneering work from a diverse group of researchers, authors, designers, product managers, data scientists, financial psychologists and science communicators who have transformed my relationship with money. My deepest gratitude is shared with fellow behavioural scientists whose groundbreaking insights have laid the foundation for this book. Their rigorous research, experiments and commitment to studying the intricacies of human behaviours have illuminated how we might improve financial wellbeing. To the content creators who have previously brought this conversation to the forefront, I extend my heartfelt gratitude for your contribution to this work. Through your engaging platforms, you have played a crucial role in making the complex world of finance less daunting. To every person who has contributed ideas to shape my own mindsets—your guidance has made the writing of this book possible.

I was fortunate to have had the opportunity to listen to the personal stories of my close, dear friends and now share them in the form of science-based narratives. The science behind the mindsets will surely evolve but the lived experiences of their stories remain unchanged. May your mindsets inspire us to enhance our individual and collective financial wellbeing.

Introduction: My first relationship with money

"Busted!" a student murmured as she passed by the corridor. I sat outside the principal's office holding fat stacks of cash in both my hands. Visualising every worst-case scenario playing on repeat in my head was making me feel dizzy. The school had notified my parents to come in soon for an urgent meeting. If you come from a similar social milieu, you might be able to relate to the guilt that I was experiencing.

Being raised by South Asian parents, I was the recipient of an abundance of love and affection. My parents held sky-high expectations for my academic and extracurricular accomplishments. They set concrete goals for me to achieve that included acing every mathematics examination and becoming an Olympics-level swimmer. Unfortunately, being summoned to the principal's office for my criminal activities did not meet any of their lofty expectations.

My crime was making too much money. As an 11-year-old, I had so much money that there was nothing left in the world that I needed to buy. My wardrobe was bursting with thirty different hats, one for each day of the month. I owned every game worth playing on the PlayStation, the entire collection of Oscar-nominated films on DVD and the latest Manchester United home and away football kits. The drinks and snacks at the school cafeteria were a steal, costing just small change. I would often 'pay it forward' by treating the next kid in line to a surprise item, long before this act of kindness turned into a viral phenomenon on social media. But I am not self-indulgent about how I made my fortune. Even after two decades, I still feel ashamed when I narrate this story. You may be wondering, "What kind of business could make an 11-year-old ridiculously rich?"

My business was about sourcing collector items and selling them to a loyal clientele of fellow students. My first supplier was a street vendor who sold posters of famous athletes and musicians. Noticing his posters were much cheaper than the ones in the bookstore near my school, I decided to test selling these celebrity posters to kids between eight and fourteen. That was my first experiment in the market. It was a roaring success.

Soon after that, I invited two of my close friends to join as business partners so we could expand the operations. Our venture took off like a rocket. We were right in the middle of all the school conversations and knew what young kids desired before Google figured it out. For our next phase of expansion, we sought out the best suppliers for other hot-ticket items like collector fountain pens, football jerseys and music merchandise from kids' favourite bands. We even hired a few classmates as runners to distribute our goods and spread the word on old-school chat forums like ICQ and MSN Messenger. The kids at school went wild for our goods. Soon, we had a loyal following that pre-ordered literally every item we dropped in the market.

So why was I standing outside the principal's office with stacks of cash? Things started to unravel when our biggest customer fell into a deep financial hole. He was stealing money from his mother to keep his credit rolling. My big mistake was introducing a 'buy now, pay later' scheme. This was long before it became a common trend in popular high street stores. Of course, I was just an 11-year-old back then when I thought it was a good idea. Many high street retailers and financial service providers still consider it a fabulous offering for their customers.

Now, we faced a crisis that would bring down our entire operation. In this boy's last transaction, he purchased twenty collector fountain pens, five original football jerseys and our entire supply of WWF trump cards for the year. Somehow, I never stopped to ask myself: "Who needs twenty fountain pens?"

Our hustle got busted! His mother had come storming into school to inform the principal that her son had been forced to steal. The cash stolen amounted to roughly the value of a hatchback car. The boy claimed that my two business partners held him on either side and the kingpin, yours truly, had wielded a knife to his throat. While I was guilty of maximising our profits at all costs, this accusation was too far removed from reality. We were just young enterprising kids selling stuff to our peers at school. None of us would ever resort to violence, or physical or verbal intimidation.

Fortunately, all three of our parents who were present in the principal's office knew that we were not capable of being that rowdy. But, the adults in the room were deeply intrigued by the fact that three kids managed to grow a company with a cash flow surpassing that of many Silicon Valley companies valued at millions of dollars around the dot-com bubble. That was a reasonable reaction considering the inflated valuations that many technology companies received at the time.

We provided a detailed account of our operations and returned all the money we had saved in cash to the boy's mother. Not long after, we moved on to more typical activities for kids like skipping school to play football and multiplayer computer games. Looking back, it's surreal to think about the first business I started with my closest friends at school. At the time, all that mattered was that we managed to get away with a one-day suspension from school. As time passed, we fondly remembered some of the projects we had undertaken in our business. One time, we commissioned a ten-year-old boy to create postcards with caricatures for the entire year. Apparently, this motivated him to pursue art for many years to follow and today he is an accomplished designer and award-winning photographer.

But as I reflect on my past, I still can't help but wonder: "Who needs twenty fountain pens?" Sure, there are some individuals who are ambidextrous and may require two writing instruments. But any realistic case for needing twenty fountain pens is a stretch for my wild imagination. I wondered whether owning twenty fountain pens may have been a way for this boy to gain social status. Since he came from a prominent business family, it's possible that he wanted to be seen as the richest kid at school. Sometimes I wonder if the passing of his wealthy father the same year may have played a role in his spending behaviour. Perhaps it was a way for him to maintain peer recognition of still being super wealthy. I may never find out the real motivation behind his actions. Be that as it may, this sparked my own curiosity about how my first relationship with money shaped how I behave with money today.

My early relationship with money has stirred a tide in me that ebbs and flows with emotions. Sometimes I feel secure in my financial position. Sometimes I feel anxious about affording to pay rent as the cost-of-living spirals upwards. Sometimes

I avoid talking about it. When I focus my attention, I visualise waves of feelings passing through my body. Often, I dip my feet in these waters, listening intently to what they are revealing to me. Occasionally, I get curious and try to bodysurf a wave. However, I draw the boundary at not letting my feelings carry me into the deep sea.

$$$

Fast forward two decades later, I founded a second business. In my behavioural science lab, headquartered in New Zealand, we help teams design products and services to improve financial wellbeing. As the Chief Behavioural Scientist, I work alongside leadership teams in technology startups, banks, financial institutions, charities and government agencies. From this vantage point, I have learned two big lessons about money.

First lesson: How we feel about money shapes how we behave with money.

This is because human behaviour is not governed by models of logical thinking. Behaviours are deeply intertwined with feelings that shape our mindsets. Renowned neuroscientist and philosopher, Antonio Damasio, has challenged the conventional wisdom that feelings are merely byproducts of the mind.[1] He argues that feelings are an essential driver of all human endeavours as they enable us to make complex decisions, inspire creativity, and form intimate social connections. For our money mindsets, feelings are not just an afterthought but a fundamental aspect of how we make everyday financial decisions.

Second lesson: What we do with money is far more important than what we know about money.

More knowledge about money does not translate into bigger savings. It's what we do with our money that matters. Small changes to our saving and spending behaviours are not always noticeable. But, just like compound interest, small changes snowball into big returns over time.

$$$

This book does not tell you to change what you do with your money. Instead, it offers mindsets to change how you think about money. The idea behind money mindsets is to become aware of why we do what we do with our money, so that we can rewire our own behaviours. The strength-based stories in this book will prompt you to reflect on your early relationship with money and how they influence your behaviour with money.

Nine money mindsets have been synthesised to facilitate your rewiring process. These insights are informed by the latest scientific knowledge in behavioural economics, evolutionary psychology, and neuroscience, integrated with ancient wisdom in yogic philosophy. This is your platform to pause and reflect on which mindsets serve you well and which ones do not (yet) serve you.

A wise person once said, "When the student is ready the teacher will appear."

I

Stories of Rita

Rita rewrites her money story

'Money scripts' are beliefs about money that we get from our families, socio-cultural environment, and significant life events. The term was introduced by financial psychologist Dr. Brad Klontz who compares our beliefs to scripts of a play that are passed down to us, from generation to generation. Often, we don't even know who the author is of our scripts. Yet, our money scripts play a crucial role in shaping our beliefs around money and how we behave today.

Meet Rita, our first character in this story. We explore her script and how she harnesses three mindsets as her superpowers to rewrite her money story. As you follow Rita's strength-based story, consider what are your own beliefs about money and how you might rewrite your own story.

Mindset 1. We are wired for curiosity

When Rita was nine, she wondered whether her parents had enough money for a family vacation. She hoped they could go on a trip together, but her parents' response was defensive: "Enough. We have enough."

At school, Rita heard her friends talk about their parents' wealth and extravagant vacations. They boasted about travelling to exotic international destinations in the school holidays. Rita's everyday lived experience was at odds with what her parents were describing. For her family, family vacations and meals at restaurants were never an option. She observed her father frugally switching off the heating, when the room was barely warm enough to sit in, without freezing. Her mother patiently waited for everyone to finish eating at the dinner table, and when they were done, she put the leftovers on a flatbread to feed herself.

From a young age through to adulthood, Rita and her sister were never brought into discussions about family savings, income, or expenses. All they were told was that money was meant to be spent on education. Questions about going on a family vacation were immediately shot down. They were left in the dark about why their parents made so many sacrifices at home. Little did Rita and her sister know at the time, their parents only wished for them to have a safe and secure financial future.

Rita's first relationship with money was puzzling, riddled with self-doubt, and anxiety about securing a stable financial future. Fortunately, her mindset of curiosity remained firmly in place. This curiosity ended up being her superpower in rewriting her own money story.

$$$

One of the greatest gifts of the human condition is that we have the ability to be conscious of our mindsets: why we do what we do when we do it. Our nervous systems are naturally wired with a mindset of curiosity. Embracing curiosity leads us to acquire the skills necessary to make more conscious choices with our money.

Rita remains a naturally curious person who enjoys asking thought provoking questions. One time, a question was posed on Reddit: "Do you believe humans should travel to Mars?" This prompted her to reflect on her personal values, the information stored in her knowledge bank and the emotional response this stirred in her. She considered the trade-offs between the long-term benefits of space exploration and short-term environmental impact. Humanity's troubled history with colonisation on our own planet was top of her mind. Thinking of the prevalence of intergenerational trauma and widespread poverty on our own planet, she noticed the discomfort she felt in her body. She responded with a question, "I wonder if space travel may amplify climate injustice on our planet?"

Ian Leslie, author of *Curious*, explains why our quest for information matters.[1] One of the big drivers for learning something new is when we encounter an 'information gap'. Celebrated authors of thriller books create an arc in their plots to keep us wanting to know what is going to happen next. Some pieces of the puzzle become clear while others are left unanswered. The information gap motivates us to keep reading more.

Complementing our curious nature, another unique trait from our evolutionary history is long-term memory. Humans are wired to move useful information from our short-term memory to our long-term bank of knowledge. However, with the emergence of new technologies and access to information at our fingertips, some may question whether it is still relevant for us to memorise poetry or read about history. After all, we can simply Google it or even write a prompt for ChatGPT to summarise all of it for us.

While we can Google everything under the sun, a crucial question remains: How do humans learn to make conscious decisions? The idea that we can synthesise an abundance of information from Wikipedia and other digital sources within seconds is immensely powerful. However, we don't really learn how to think by merely asking ChatGPT to summarise ideas. We learn how to think consciously about a topic when we hear concepts multiple times, in different situations, repeated in unique contexts, through reading it in poetry, conversations with family, and asking questions.

From Rita's question on Reddit, we can see how conscious thinking is the result of curiosity in a wide range of topics. The same is true with the topic of money.

$$$

Should we choose a weekly or annual gym membership? Is it

better to invest our savings in Exchange traded funds (ETFs) or cryptocurrency? Should we pay a fee for a credit card with reward points or a free debit card? There are thousands of conscious decisions that we need to make with our money. Curiosity is our superpower to navigate this intricate web of choices.

One psychological phenomenon that we ought to be curious about is: pain of paying. The term was coined in a 1996 dissertation paper.[2] It refers to the negative emotions we experience during a transaction when we part with our money. The evidence showed that people preferred the least painful payment methods, such as credit cards, over the most painful method, which was cash. Follow-up studies have demonstrated how paying with cash provides instant gratification, whereas paying with a credit card delays the pain of parting with our money. This is until our future selves have to pay the bill.

Ramifications of this for our future selves span across other contexts, such as eating healthier foods. In one experiment, people who paid for groceries with credit cards were more likely to purchase junk food, such as candy, sugary drinks, and fast food.[3] With contactless payment options like Google Pay, Apple Pay, AliPay, and Amazon's 'Just Walk Out Technology', it's incredibly easy and painless to spend money. While we can now simply walk out of these Amazon stores without having to even stop to make a payment, more convenience also means less savings. A little bit of friction may just be what we need to balance our saving and spending decisions.

One way that we can introduce some obstacles into our spending habits is by adopting the zero-based budgeting system. In this system, we spend all our money on expenses every month so that the amount left in the bank account is zero. How does this help us save more and spend less? The trick is to include savings like emergency funds, investments and other saving goals as part of our expenses. We can even set up different accounts in our bank for different types of expenses, such as rent, food, utility bills, entertainment, repaying debt and saving goals. This may help us make more deliberate choices with our money.

Should we avoid contactless payments in order to leverage our psychological pain of paying response? Is it worth opening multiple accounts with our bank to curb the impact of easy payments? How can we leverage the latest science-based tools to make more conscious money decisions?

Asking more questions is the antidote to our money challenges. We don't need to have all the answers just yet. This is where our innate drive for curiosity will fill the information gaps that we start to create.

$$$

Children between 3 to 5 years old ask around 300 questions per day.[1] The single biggest factor that determines their level of curiosity is how it is received by people around them. If a child is met with stony silence when they frantically gesture at something, they abandon the exploration. When they are met with patience and openness the seeds of curiosity are planted. Children whose parents encourage questions are better at acquiring language and staying curious later on as adults.

Consider the variance in mindsets of two children from the same classroom. The first child comes from a so-called cognitively rich household. These are families where the parents have time and money to facilitate more early learning. They have resources like books and encyclopaedias around their house, with time to read and share stories with their children. They have more bandwidth to play with their children and build their curiosity. The second child doesn't have the same privilege and baseline level of general knowledge of the world around them. They may live in a home without sufficient heating, with a single parent working double shifts, six days a week just to get enough food on the table. Their mental and emotional faculties reflect those of their primary caregiver and are thus in more of a survival mode.

The first child with a head-start will acquire new information at a faster rate. This child will most likely get further and further ahead. There is a compounding effect. It is more difficult to learn about a new subject if we don't have information stored in our long-term memory. The second child may find school incredibly challenging. The education system may make them feel inferior for not learning at the same pace. They may feel higher education is not suited for them. This heartbreaking scenario is rife across schools today. This can be likened to the 'rich get richer' phenomenon. The longer it goes on, the wider the gap and the more difficult it becomes for any external factor to level the playing field.

Children who turn out to be curious adults live in households where their parents frequently speak to them. These parents respond to their children's queries with questions like: "I think it means this, but I'm not sure. What do you think?"

The key principle to understand about curiosity is that it works like a muscle. To keep the connection of curiosity strong, we have to work on it. Doing a regular work-out pays off in the long run. Having a broader base of knowledge means that we can learn more and take pleasure in learning.

$$$

Curiosity can take effort and time, and in the internet age, it can sometimes take us down a rabbit hole when we have more pressing tasks to do. To effectively engage in sustained learning, it is important to combine both diversity curiosity and epistemic curiosity. Diversity curiosity helps us to familiarise ourselves with basic information and gain new and novel input, while epistemic curiosity allows us to gain specialised knowledge on a subject.

Diversity curiosity is characterised by a craving for new input, novelty, and excitement. It is a behaviour that is motivating, impulsive, and hard to resist all at once. Here's a forum from Reddit demonstrating this type of curiosity.

> Question: "What's the best YouTube rabbit hole you've been in?"
>
> Response: MRE unboxing vids. Basically there is this fairly big channel I found randomly who opens and tastes military food ration from all around the world in a very serious and passionate way. You never see the face of the guy and that's a plus for me since I don't like looking at people eating, and the sounds of the metallic tray and cans are incredibly soothing. He even tries bags of sealed MRE from the 80's sometimes" — RE_DELLA_MERDA via Reddit

Epistemic curiosity, on the other hand, requires conscious choice, focus, and attention. It goes deeper and takes more work to sustain this type of curiosity, which is seen in artists deeply involved in their creation process or PhD students conducting research for years on a specific topic. Reading a book involves effort and is central to the practice of epistemic curiosity. Despite the abundance of information available in the digital age, there is value in acquiring knowledge through slow and intentional practices like reading.

One strategy for selecting books to read is clustering our reading topics. As recommended by polymath and blogger Tyler Cohen, this strategy involves obtaining maps of information from various sources on a related topic. It helps the information stick in our long-term memory and enhances our ability to engage in deeper critical thinking. For instance, if we want to develop new money-saving habits, we could cluster reading books such as *Good Money* by Nathalie Spencer, *The Power of Habit* by Charles Duhigg, and *How to Change* by Kathy Milkman.

A wide base of knowledge with deep pockets in certain domains is essential to the creative process. Unrelated thoughts and ideas serve as the breeding ground for creativity to emerge. The wider the base and deeper the pockets, the more unrelated connections we can make.

$$\$\$\$$

Starting rich does not mean finishing rich.

The STAR program is designed for successful individuals, including athletes at George Washington University who are enrolled in this special M.B.A. programme. Professor Annamaria Lusardi, who teaches economics and accountancy at the school, describes them as very talented and competent.[4] Many of these individuals come from backgrounds where they were not taught the basics of financial literacy. In particular, many professional football players who are part of this program have significant wealth and reputations to manage.

Lusardi and her colleagues conducted a study on a cohort of NFL players who were drafted in the late 1990s and early 2000s to assess their long-term financial outcomes.[5] Despite the median length of a career being just six years, N.F.L. players earned more than the average college graduate would earn in their entire lifetime. Yet 15 percent of these players went bankrupt. This is at a rate that's even higher than the overall population of men in their age group and despite the fact that the NFL retirees had already earned a career's worth of income. Professor Lusardi found that the risk of bankruptcy did not decline for the players who earned the most. They simply could not translate the lump sum they had earned into a resource that they could support themselves with during their lifetime.

The world of money is complex, and making an informed decision involves learning about inflation, interest rates, retirement savings, mutual funds, insurance, cryptocurrency and much more. Being wired for curiosity can equip us to better understand this complex world. Children who are asked more questions tend to ask more questions in return. This is also true for adults. Channelling our mindsets for curiosity can help us ask the money questions that matter the most to us.

Pause and reflect:

1. *Start with asking one question you have about money.*
2. *How can you add friction to make more conscious choices with your money?*
3. *Remember that curiosity works like a muscle, use it or lose it.*

4. *To go further in rewiring your money mindsets, ask wider questions about related topics, such as behaviour change, habits and the science of well being.*
5. *The skills to earn money are different from the skills to save money.*

Mindset 2. Framing your own money story

Rita dreams of starting a family. She wants to live with the security of her own home where she can turn it into a nurturing space. She wishes to have a garden to tend to, turning food scraps into fine compost, and growing cherry tomatoes in the richness of the soil microbiome.

She told a friend, "I want to dedicate my time and energy to creating a homely space, where my family and plants can thrive, without the constant threats of rent hikes or eviction from my landlady." Rita enjoys spending her time surfing on her longboard, making her own lasagne from scratch and going on multi-day tramps in the outdoors. Her dream house is walking distance from a beach. It has a spacious bathtub, where she can unwind after a long day, and a fireplace to sit around, sipping a hot cacao beverage on a cold winter day.

She aspires to start her own physiotherapy practice so that she can be more flexible with her time. In this work, she wants to offer help to underserved communities who may not be able to afford her services. But, she is aware that providing free support one day a week will enrich her own wellbeing too. Being drawn to authenticity, she wishes to build more lasting relationships in her local community. The small actions of giving and receiving bring her joy. She would like to embrace this principle of reciprocity that she learned from plants.

This is the story of Rita.

$$$

Don't think of an elephant!

We are often drawn to negative stories, more than the positive ones. This serves us well from an evolutionary standpoint. We are constantly vigilant and aware of potential threats in order to remain safe and secure.

But this feature of the human mind doesn't serve us well when it comes to avoiding thinking of an elephant. Neither does it serve us well in 'asset-framing' or the subtle art of framing our own positive stories.

> *"Asset-framing is a direct expression of the love doctrine, right? It is defining people by their aspirations and contributions, before you get to their challenges." — Trabian Shorters (founder and CEO of the BMe Community)*

To understand asset-framing, we need to call in the opposite. This is the default operating model for many of us in the world: deficit-framing. We have a habit of seeing problems and defining people in need of support in terms of their challenges. Very often, we focus on people's vulnerabilities and how the world is stacked against them. We may say people are 'at-risk' of something bad or belong to a 'low socio-economic group'.

We're framing people with these labels. But people don't carry these labels when they face the world.

Take a positive story from the world of microfinance as an example. This radical experiment was the brainchild of Bangladeshi Nobel Peace Prize winner and economist Mohammed Yunus. His work shows how people who are underserved by banking services, can be recognised for their strengths by other non-banking financial companies.

Microfinance organisations give customers access to small loans even though they do not have collateral to secure a loan. Here's the most fascinating part of this experiment. The repayment rates for the unsecured loans are much higher than the average repayment rates for loans. These so-called unsecured loans are given to people who do not have assets, such as property or investments, to secure loans from a traditional bank. In other words, people who did not have assets to offer as security were more likely to pay back their loans.

The invisible strengths in a community can easily go unnoticed as an asset. In many cases, loans were given to women only. Practice-based evidence with the community revealed that women were more responsible at managing the household finances. Men in the household were lured to spending money on alcohol or gambling through social pressure and targeted advertising campaigns. Crucially, the loan is handed out to a group of women. Typically, a group of ten women were jointly responsible for paying back the entire sum of money. Some households needed cash flow for their small business. Others needed money to pay for day-to-day household expenses.

If one woman had difficulty repaying their share of the loan, a woman from another household covers for them. They do all they can to support their households and each other in the group as one unit. This strong sense of group accountability and reciprocity were some of the invisible strengths of the community. This is a safe and secure asset.

Asset-framing is about not framing people by their challenges. This does not mean that systemic challenges should not be the focus of our attention. But if we start to define ourselves by our aspirations, rather than our vulnerabilities, what we are framing is the true story of who we really are.

If we don't start with the dreams that people have, we make people a target object. Our focus becomes about persuading people to change their lifestyles. We may engage with people or ourselves as problems that need fixing. As Trabian Shorters points out: "When we do this, we need to recognise that we've become part of the problem."

We all have dreams and aspirations. This may involve living sustainably in a home with a beautiful garden or providing our children the best possible education so they can have a secure financial future.

$$\$\$\$$$

"Everything is based on mind, is led by mind, is fashioned by mind." — *Gautama Buddha*

This is from the opening chapter of the Dhammapada. A timeless collection of Buddha's sayings. The word "dhamma" can be thought of as wisdom and "pada" can be thought of as the path in this context. Of course, literal translations from the sacred language Pāli, native to the Indian subcontinent, does not map directly onto Western language and worldviews.

As renowned Canadian physician Dr. Gabor Maté explains: the world we believe in becomes the world we live in. If we see the world as a hostile place where winners take all, we may become selfish and aggressive to survive in such an environment. Later in life, we may gravitate towards competitive endeavours that confirm this view and reinforces this worldview. Our beliefs are not only self-fulfilling, but they build our worldview.

Building on this, Gabor eloquently says, "Before the mind can create the world, the world creates our minds." His trauma-informed research explores how people who have experienced trauma have a worldview tinged with fear, pain and suspicion. This lens can distort and determine our view of reality. In other cases, a naively rosy perspective may emerge, through the forces of denial, that blind us to real and present dangers.

In the book *Useful Delusions*, NPR's social science correspondent Shankar Vedantam discusses this subjective nature of our reality.[1] Our eyes alone take in about a billion bits of information at any moment. If all this information was transmitted to the brain, we would get overwhelmed with an enormous sensory overload. By filtering in 1 out of 1000 bits, we pass on a million bits to the brain and then process around 40 bits of this information. Starting with a billion bits, our brain processes just 40 bits of information. This is how we have learned to make sense in a world of plentiful stimuli.

For decades, people believed that if you have depression or anxiety, you are seeing the world with a delusional pessimism. Shankar points out many recent studies that have terminated this notion and find the opposite to be true. People coping with depression are often just seeing the world more accurately. This is the story of who they really are and part of their invisible strengths.

$$$

There is a quirk about human perception that will change how you think about medicine—and money. It's the reason why a placebo can reduce pain.

A more expensive painkiller can work better at reducing pain. In a famous study, the exact same pill at $2.50 provided more relief than one that cost only 10 cents.[2] The higher price created a better impression of efficacy. It can be near impossible to break such hardwired expectations. Sometimes it is easier to change reality than it is to change expectations. Placebos take advantage of the fact that the brain doesn't want to divert from beliefs.

For the healthcare industry, they are more than just sugar pills. All the theatre surrounding medicine contributes to our belief that we will feel better.[3] For example, people respond better when they physically see the physician administering the medication. This medication works better compared to instances where patients do not see the medicine being loaded to the intravenous (IV) for treatment. The theatre around medicine involves white lab coats and this is something that we ought to celebrate as a strength of the human condition.

The nervous system can simulate the experience of feeling better, which becomes part of our wiring, both physically and psychologically. The stories we frame for ourselves are a part of our reality.

This is what it means to be human!

$$$

When it comes to framing your money story, focussing on the good that we are already doing is a vital step. If we share an aspiration like Rita, we are doing really well. This can be viewed as a strength to move towards something tangible.

If we are saving money or paying our credit card bills on time, we are already on our way to financial stability. Many financial experts encourage people to treat themselves while doing their financial planning or budgeting. If we treat ourselves while planning our financial future, we are likely to feel good about revisiting this plan in the future. This may be the motivation we need to plan for long-term financial dreams.

While financial dreams can be the motivation we need to get started, life almost always gets in the way. Researchers found that assigning a "get out of jail free card" can help people persist with things after failure.[4] In one study, 315 participants tracked their step count for five weeks. They were randomly assigned to one of four groups. Two groups had optional emergency skips in case they missed a day. The researchers found that the groups with emergency skips had achieved their step count more days per week on average. The "get out of jail free" cards can prepare us for changing life circumstances.

We can't expect ourselves to be 100% all of the time. We can't control external forces that impact our situation. But we can frame a story for ourselves that makes space for self-compassion.

$$\$\$\$$$

Can reframing beliefs change our outcomes?

In 2007, Dr. Alia Crum (Director of the Stanford Mind & Body

Lab) and Ellen Langer (Professor of Psychology at Harvard University) wanted to research this very question.[5]

To test this, they searched for a group of people who get plenty of exercise. They found this in an unlikely place: hotels. The subjects were not the guests on vacation. It turned out that the housekeepers in the hotel were actually getting plenty of exercise simply by showing up to their job each day. Cleaning hotel rooms is a very physically demanding job. However, many of the housekeeping staff did not view their work as exercise. They assumed that the work they were putting in was just hard, painful work.

The researchers evaluated what would happen if they changed the framing to view work as good exercise. They hypothesised that if staff viewed themselves as getting enough exercise, they were more likely to receive more benefits. To evaluate this, they randomised 84 housekeeping staff into two groups.

One group was told that their work counted as good exercise. Further, they were told that it satisfied the US Surgeon General's recommendations for a healthy lifestyle so they should expect to see the benefits of their physical work. The other group was the control group and were not provided this information.

The researchers found that women who reframed their work as exercise dropped blood pressure and body fat. This was significantly more than the control group who hadn't made this frame.

Framing our beliefs seems to matter for outcomes. A lot more than we may believe.

$$$

There is a long tradition of faith healing in Mexico City. This was the location where award-winning science journalist Erik Vance was writing his book, aptly titled *Suggestible You.* One of the places he ended up in for his research was San Pablito, a mountain town in Puebla. The mystical town, which almost hangs off a mountain, has a history of curanderos who practise shamanic healing with a firm root in indigenous knowledge.

Erik describes an instance where he went to see a native healer in San Pablito. He had an ongoing issue with his knee that he attributed to ageing. The healer performed an elaborate ritual that involved burning some herbs and wrapping her mouth around his knee. This seemed absurd at the time, but since he had been researching the placebo effect, he knew the importance of keeping an open belief. When he was sent away, Erik noticed that the pain in his knee had significantly reduced, and he was able to walk up and down steep steps without any pain. Despite his scepticism as a science writer, he knew this feeling was real. Whether it was a placebo or not, he experienced a relief in his pain.

What Erik was most interested in was the power of his beliefs to change his own outcomes. They are not one-off cases limited to the powers of shamanistic healers. We all have the power to change our own stories.

In the context of medical trials, the control group is given a sugar pill. No one knows whether they are receiving the placebo or not. This procedure rules out inaccurate reports about any improvements simply because they are receiving some treatment. If one group is given a sugar pill, and the other does not receive any pill, people with the placebo typically experience some of the benefits of treatment. This is the real power of the placebo effect in all of us.

Our stories influence how we feel. When we feel we are getting good exercise, we feel better physically and psychologically. Our money story impacts our spotlight of focus. What we believe to be true about the world changes what we pay attention to. Being aware of your financial dreams and aspirations can make the hard sacrifices we make feel more than worthwhile.

The most important thing about money stories is to simply accept that they exist. We're always filtering the world through our own psychological lenses. Our money story is framed with a wide range of pre-existing assumptions, beliefs and expectations.

When we start to reframe our money story, a whole new reality opens up for us.

Pause and reflect:

1. *Identify three of your financial dreams and aspirations.*
2. *What are your invisible strengths with money that people don't notice?*
3. *Recognise something you are doing well in your financial life.*
4. *How can self-compassion enable you to persist with your long-term goals?*
5. *You can change your financial outcomes by framing your own money story.*

Mindset 3. Nudge the system!

Rita adopted a system to save money from early childhood. In fact, she was nudged to do this. On her tenth birthday, Rita's grandmother opened a savings account with 20 dollars in her name, giving her a gentle push towards becoming a great saver in adulthood. From a young age, Rita's parents emphasised the importance of saving money too, but they never discussed it in the language of a money script or explained why being financially independent would benefit her in the future. Instead, they modelled saving behaviours through their everyday actions. Looking back, Rita recognises that the saving behaviours her parents modelled were her money scripts that served her well.

During her college years, Rita attended a prestigious university in New York City, where she learned to survive on a student budget, in one of the most expensive cities in the world. Later, she pursued graduate school to become a physiotherapist. After completing her studies, she landed a well-paying job at a private practice, rehabilitating athletes. For the first time in her life, she had money to put aside. Occasionally, Rita spent more than she did during her college days on international travel and yoga classes. Later on, she took a lower-paying job at a community health centre. Despite changes in her life circumstances, Rita managed to consistently save money by instructing her bank to automatically deposit 10% of any new income into her savings account. After trying a few different systems, this was something that worked for her.

Over the last twenty years, the bank account that Rita's grandmother opened for her was the little nudge that made saving money easy and automatic.

$$\$\$\$$$

How might we nudge the system so that it works for us? Imagine if we can design our own systems on our mobile banking app or financial technology (aka fintech companies) app to reach our financial dreams and aspirations. A puzzle the financial industry needs to address is how they can design products and services to enable this.

The classic case of retirement savings highlights how automatic pension enrollment has become widespread in many countries. Instead of actively opting in, employees are automatically enrolled in the workplace pension scheme, with the option to opt-out if they choose to do so. Research indicates that participation rates rose from 49% to 86% for employees automatically enrolled in the system.[1] A more recent study with better quality data has demonstrated an even higher uptake in participation.

The concept of 'nudge' highlights these potential system-level changes on individual behaviour. Coined by behavioural economist Richard Thaler and legal scholar Cass Sunstein, in their namesake book, *Nudge* showcased how small changes in the way we present choices to people can have a big impact on the decisions we make. This can be achieved without banning options or significantly changing incentives.

Let's take the example of addictive mobile phones. Many of us struggle with the temptation to aimlessly scroll through our mobile at night. To overcome this temptation, Arianna Huffington (founder CEO of Thrive Global) developed a behaviourally-informed product: the Phone Bed Charging Station. This is a dedicated space where the entire family can tuck their phones into bed at night. Now instead of battling this temptation alone, we can make a commitment as a family to support each other with this troublesome behaviour. As a bonus, we get our devices fully charged in the morning. We are not banned from using the mobile at night, but there is some level of social accountability from family members to adopt this new behaviour.

Can financial innovators design systems like the Phone Bed Charging Station?

$$$

The combination of behavioural science and human-centred design has been leveraged by industry disruptors to support people to save money on mobile apps. This technology has the potential to improve the financial wellbeing of millions of customers. There is a massive opportunity for mainstream banks and emerging fintech companies to develop more behaviourally-informed products and services.

"You do not rise to the level of your goals. You fall to the level of your systems" — James Clear

Founder of the Irrational Retirement blog, Žiga Vižintin co-authored an article on this topic.[2] Imagine every time you spend $100 at the supermarket, the bank automatically moves $20 to your retirement savings account. This "saving-through-spending" system is an innovative way financial services and tech companies are working together alongside the government to help people save money for the future. He highlights that system changes reach people who are typically underserved by the banking sector, such as students, freelancers, small businesses and those who are informally employed.

One of his best proof points that saving-through-spending programs can work is: Miles for Retirement in Mexico. For context, they are a financial services provider that generates the most voluntary retirement savings in the whole of Mexico. Their mobile app is connected to the user's credit or debit card. When registering, every member defines the percentage to automatically save from their own account in relation to how much they spend. For example, if you set 5% and bought $100 worth of groceries at the store, $5 would be automatically transferred from your checking account into your retirement savings account. Once the money is in your retirement account, it is invested in one of the dedicated low-cost retirement saving funds, which are managed by private pension funds. After it's set up, the app is on autopilot and tucks away savings into your retirement account every time you shop.

From banks to fintech companies, the evidence is clear. The secret sauce behind saving money is pretty basic: make it easy and automatic. These are the psychological levers that we can adopt for a reliable system that saves our money too.

$$$

Many of us wish to eat healthily, exercise more and save money for the future. As you may know from experience, this is easier said than done.

When it comes to temptation, we can think of humans as having two selves—the present self and the future self. If you have ever set goals for yourself, like new year's resolutions to go for a run three times a week, you may find yourself in the company of most people who fail to stick with them. Behavioural scientists have illustrated how humans prefer smaller rewards in the present over larger rewards in the future. Sticking to good behaviours is hard because the present self—by definition—is the person who is presently in control of our decisions. If our present selves desire a donut, there is no stopping us from enjoying it.

Professor Katherine Milkman and her colleagues at Wharton Business School conducted a study with an online grocery.[3] This revealed that people purchased more 'want' items, such as ice-cream and donuts, when the delivery time was short. But with longer delivery times, people spent more on healthy items, like vegetables and fruits that were great for their future selves.

We have a 'marshmallow brain' as popularised by the famous marshmallow experiment. This is a brain that focuses on instant rewards and short-term gratification. But this experiment does not replicate or even tell the full story of human potential.

We also have what philosopher Roman Krznaric refers to as the 'akon brain'.[4] This part of the brain is dedicated to long-term decision-making. We have the capacity to save for our children's education, voyage into space exploration, and in some instances, we chose the playlist for our own funeral. Human beings are extremely gifted at planning for the future too.

Just like Rita, many of us have the capacity to save money too. All we need to do is nudge the system! In other words, we can design a system that enables us to become good at saving more and spending less.

$$$

Our banks can nudge the system for us!

ASB Bank in New Zealand has a behaviourally-informed service called 'Save the Change'. When a customer spends money, it tucks away the change into your savings account. So every time you spend $4.60 on a coffee, 40 cents goes to your future self. You simply set the default to round up your transaction to the nearest multiple of $1, $2, $5 or $10.

It helps customers save, especially when they don't have the bandwidth to think about it. This feature makes savings more accessible to many more people.

Our present selves may want to spend, but our future selves may have long-term financial goals. Nobel laureate and be-havioural economist Richard Thaler has a mantra: "If you want people to do something, make it easy." If we want to support people to eat healthy, then replace the junk food with healthy food at the supermarket checkout counter. Similarly, if we want to help people to save for their future selves, then make it easy and automatic.

Studies estimated that around half the UK population has a savings bank account. At a Ted conference, Rory Sutherland (Ogilvy UK vice-chairman and co-founder of Ogilvy Consult-ing's behavioural science practice) made the case for making 'impulse savings' easy.

When you receive your paycheck, there is no shortage of options to spend your money. Impulse shopping is as easy as a click of a button since your card details are already stored on the website. Paying for drinks on a night out has never been easier with a tap of your card. But why isn't impulse saving easy or even provided as an option for many of us?

In the mantra of ideas worth spreading, this inspired fellow creative agency Colenso to partner with Westpac Bank to make saving as easy as spending. This was more of a concept, but they launched it in the Apple App Store. Now bank customers could add up to $50 to their savings account at the push of a button. When the paycheck comes in, customers have an easy alternative to make an impulse saving.

$$$

Unfortunately, not all banks have systems in place that put their customers' wellbeing at the centre of decision-making.

Profit models and incentives in the industry create a plethora of financial products and services that fail to serve the best interests of their customers. Despite the widespread belief that financial education is to blame for low savings rates, even financially savvy customers find it incredibly challenging to save money. This situation leaves most customers helpless in navigating the complex world of finance, perpetuating a culture of blame. Social media companies like Instagram and TikTok deploy behavioural science nudges to keep us hooked on their platform. There is a risk that our banking and financial service providers may adopt similar strategies that do not align with our long-term financial goals.

For banks and fintech companies that aim to support customers to make better personal financial choices, it is important to recognise that no one-size-fits-all solution exists. We all have different financial goals and risk tolerances, and we are unique individuals with our own money stories. To empower people to make better choices with money, we need systems that enable us to become the choice architects of our own lives.[5] This is how we can nudge the system to work for us.

As the proverb goes: give a human a fish and you feed this person for a day; teach this human to fish and you feed this person for a lifetime.

Pause and reflect:

1. *How can you use technology to spend less and save more money?*
2. *If you have systems that make it easy to save money, you are far more likely to follow through with this intention.*
3. *What nudges can you create in your immediate environment to help you save small amounts more frequently?*
4. *How can you flip the impulse to spend money into an impulse to save money?*
5. *While financial service providers ought to design better system-level nudges, you are the best architect for designing your own individual-level nudge.*

II

Stories of Rodri

Rodri reroutes his money compass

In the beginning, Rodri worked diligently, repaying student loans without any concrete goals in mind. Then, his life took a turn when he rerouted his money compass. The metaphor of a money compass refers to a set of guiding principles that help us stay on track with our financial goals. Enabled by each of the three mindsets described in this story, his analog compass transformed into a digital compass.

After gaining a sense of purpose, Rodri needed his compass to point to a new north star as the destination. But he realised that 'north' in his money compass always pointed in the same direction. Rodri got a digital compass that enabled him to set his true north. Next, he downloaded a new feature that allowed him to enter coordinates in his digital compass that accurately guided him with pinpoint accuracy. A software upgrade to the digital compass provided him real-time feedback. This showed him how much progress he was making towards his destination.

Similar to the various routes offered by the GPS on Google Maps, the developing human brain has multiple potential connections to enable the same behaviour. With repeated actions, some neural pathways are reinforced while others gradually diminish. These pathways, established until roughly the age of 25, pave the route for default behaviours.

The phenomenon of one-trial learning can occur early in our childhood. For example, a child who almost drowns in the ocean may immediately develop a fear of swimming. But this negative experience does not mean that the child cannot learn to swim later in life. Rather, they can reconfigure their relationship with water by engaging in exposure therapy or joining a trusted partner in a swimming pool. By setting small goals and celebrating progress along the way, this person can rewire their default behaviours and become confident swimmers in the open sea.

Neuroscience has taught us that "neurons that fire together wire together." Throughout early childhood, we learn to reinforce essential connections while pruning irrelevant ones to cater to our emotional requirements. This wiring process ultimately moulds our behaviours as adults. Yet, similar to how a child can acquire swimming skills later in life, we have the capacity to reroute our money compass.

Mindset 4. Power of visualisation

Rodri's parents got divorced when he was four years old. Both Rodri and his younger brother were raised by his mother, who was still a PhD student when she separated from his father. His mother is now an associate professor of psychology at a community college. But the financial struggles during his early childhood remain etched in his memory.

His uncle and grandfather worked as lumber cutters. They started work at 5 AM and finished working at sundown. At the age of fourteen, Rodri got his first job as an apprentice in the lumber business. He vowed never to end up with the same financial struggle he experienced growing up. Throughout high school, he worked summer holidays, and he continued to chop wood when he was studying in university. He made enough money to support his own education. Rodri marvelled at the connection between the inner workings of the human mind and the natural world. Like his mother, he was interested in psychology. He completed his bachelor's degree with a double major in Psychology and International Relations.

When he graduated from university, Rodri did not see himself getting a job in an office. His model of the world was disjointed. While his peers got internships in international development agencies and management consultancies, he worked long hours chopping wood. The only way he knew how to make money was through physical work. The idea of sitting behind a computer doing desk research and getting paid seemed like a dystopian science fiction film.

Then, Rodri found the first part of his money compass. It came as a visualisation in a dream. He was surrounded by trees under the night sky. They were all connected via a complex network of bioluminescent fungi. Through the guardians of the underworld, the trees were speaking with each other, and they were exchanging nutrients. This resulted in a more resilient natural ecosystem in the forests where he once chopped wood. He imagined how he might become a guardian and protect the forests too. In this dream, he realised that he needed to see the planet first to discover where he was needed as a protector. After saving enough money to travel, Rodri quit working as a lumber cutter and started to travel the world.

$$$

Vision is the dominant sense by which we navigate the world. There is more real estate in the brain for vision than every other sensory input combined. This is what enables us to spot the international space station hundreds of miles away and marvel at bioluminescent algae in the ocean. Rarely do we have the experience of our eyes getting things wrong. This is why visual illusions like 'the dress' go viral on social media. It defies all of our previous expectations. We look at the sensory inputs in our everyday world without doubting whether they are real. As they say, "seeing is believing".

In the book *Dollars and Sense*, behavioural economist Dan Ariely and financial comedian Jeff Kreisler delve into how vision impacts our financial choices too.[1] Two thousand years ago, people saved their income in goats, cattle, or chickens. When people saved their earnings in livestock, they could see exactly how much the neighbours were saving. Returning home every day, they were reminded how many goats the neighbour had accumulated. This visual reminder would set up their benchmark for a good savings rate. But with the invention of money, and then digital money, it has become harder for us to visualise what we need to save for later. We lost the visual reminder from the neighbours next door. Now, we can only see what others spend their money on. We can see what cars our neighbours buy and how many people are having avocado toast on a Sunday afternoon at the local cafe.

We have two choices we can make with our money: spending and saving. Today, one of them is completely invisible i.e. saving. One of them is very visible i.e. spending. Which one are we going to focus on?

$$$

The power of visualisation is incredible.

At New York University's psychology department, Emily Balcetis has done some compelling research on this topic. A physical therapist once invited Emily to an old armoury building in Brooklyn. Here she was introduced to a coach in the team training some of the fastest runners in the world.

She asked them what strategies they use. Adopting a narrow tunnel vision strategy on the goal, they assumed hyper focussed attention on the finish line. If the finish line was a long distance away, they selected sub goals like a lamp post in front of them.

As they reached the sub goal, they picked the next target to focus their visual attention towards. Olympian long-distance runners have since revealed they use this same visualisation strategy. This narrows their attention as they are pulled toward this goal. It's almost like a spotlight is shining on the target they select. There are blinders put on to anything else that might distract them as they hone in on the next target.

Emily Balcetis wondered whether other people might be able to leverage this visualisation strategy for reaching their physical fitness goals. In a series of experiments, Emily's lab got participants to focus their visual attention on a finish line. They then engage in a behaviour that requires effort. When people focussed their visual attention on this one point, they were more likely to reach their goals. In one of her experiments, a group of people exercised with 15-pound ankle weights.[2] One group was told to visually focus on the finish line and the other group was not given this strategy. They found that the group that focussed on the goal was able to finish 23% quicker. More interestingly, this group reported 17% less effort in reaching the goal.

Visualising a goal line does something to both our psychology and physiology that allows us to move faster—and with less effort too. It's like having a destination to focus on takes away our attention from the struggles that we encounter during our journey to get there.

$$$

Have you ever wondered why a panoramic view is so rewarding?

There are few things in life that can match the experience of an endless unbroken view from atop a mountain or skyscraper. A panoramic view engages one part of our visual system which is called the magno-cellar pathway. It is involved in taking global information around us. It promotes a deep sense of relaxation to the nervous system. The act of visualising something as near or far can change our autonomic nervous system. This is the part of our nervous system that is related to involuntary body processes. It prepares us either for a state of action or sets us up for relaxation.

On the other hand, bringing our visual attention to a fixed point engages the opposite branch of our visual system. This makes our attention work like a high-definition camera. A certain set of neural circuits evaluates small changes in the focal point that we are looking at. Inducing the vision of proximity on a fixed point has several downstream psychological effects. A primary one is belief in our own ability to achieve a goal, spurring our internal dopamine circuits in the pursuit of this reward. This is neuroscience's explanation for why marathon runners pick a fixed point in the distance.[3]

One fixed point that Rodri gets pulled towards is the smell of baked goods. When he passes his local bakery, the impulse to buy an almond croissant is almost irresistible. It captures his attention and anything else that he had planned for the day becomes secondary. Immediately, this brings his spotlight of attention to the treat in his proximity. He finds it extremely challenging to resist this temptation. On some occasions, Rodri tells himself that he could buy this treat on his way back home. His attention is then back on track for purchasing groceries at the farmer's market and all the fresh produce that awaits him. He continues listening to his podcast which he zoned out of for the last sixty seconds.

The dopamine reward system doesn't work as well for long-term goals. When Rodri pushes his purchase decision out to later in the day, or the next week, the almond croissant doesn't seem half as attractive. It is not as salient or tangible as a croissant calling him in the present moment. There's a phenomenon in behavioural economics called: hyperbolic discounting. The further out in time we get a reward, the less motivating it will be in influencing our behaviour. In short, goals for our future selves are less rewarding.

A very common long-term goal many of us struggle with is saving money. We tend to imagine our future selves as another person. This makes it difficult to prioritise present decisions that serve our future wellbeing, such as saving for retirement.

$$\$\$\$$

How can we better empathise with our future selves?

This has been a central research question for Hal Hershfield, Professor of Behavioral Decision Making at UCLA, over the last two decades. His most influential work has demonstrated that many of us imagine the future self as if it is another person. It's not truly a separate person because we ultimately turn into this person. But as an analogy it captures a fundamental aspect of human nature.

Professor Hershfield speculates that this trait may have been helpful from an evolutionary perspective.[4] In the past, we needed to think about the immediate term and perhaps a couple of months out. But the concept of retirement was only invented in the last blink of an eye in evolutionary terms. With the extra decades of life expectancy, we now have to grapple with older and more distant versions of ourselves. This leads to a disconnect. It's also just easier to pay attention to things that are right in front of us.

The dilemma is that we need to make a choice between what we might want right now and what we think we might need in the future. If we don't empathise with our future selves, it is harder to prioritise decisions that we make on behalf of this person. The research demonstrates that people have better financial wellbeing when they are emotionally bonded to their future selves. The more people relate with and connect to their future selves, the more likely they are to save resources for later in life too.

One strategy is to try to make those future selves more vivid and more visual. These more vivid examples are emotional and emotional stories tend to ignite us to change current behaviours. In some of Professor Hershfield's earlier research, one group in the experiment was exposed to images of their future selves. Another group would just see an image of their current selves. They found that the people who saw the images of their future selves allocated more money to a long-term savings investment. After this groundbreaking research, Hal Hershfield and his collaborators recently wrapped up a study looking at a set of almost 50,000 consumers in Mexico. Half of them received the opportunity to view their aged selves, and half of them did not. Those who did were more likely to make a contribution to their personal pensions for retirement.

The key takeaway message is: If we can implement exercises that connect us with our future selves, that's when we can balance being more present to both our daily wants and future needs.

$$$

Nobel laureate Daniel Kahneman observed: It seems like nothing is ever as important as what you're doing right now. This is a general principle that plays out in many aspects of our lives.

We may experience this when we have a deadline for a work report or when we're watching a penalty shootout with our friends. Everything we do right now feels more important because it's right in front of us. Our visual perception is what anchors our goal-directed behaviours. What we see is principally important to what we do in the immediate term. This is why we need to focus our visual attention on our big life goals.

What does science say about visualising big goals? Is thinking about our dream home effective in helping us save money?

It turns out that it is, but we have to be careful about when and how we implement the visualisation. If done correctly, it can serve our goal-directed behaviours well. If done incorrectly, it can undermine the entire process. Here's one experiment explaining the key mechanisms at play.[5] People were told to imagine the long-term goals they wished to achieve. They were asked to script out how getting this big win is going to make them feel and note this experience with a rich amount of detail. Measuring people's blood pressure and physiology, there was excitement and a ramping up of readiness towards that goal. But that increase in blood pressure quickly waned.

Visualising the big goal is effective in getting the goal pursuit started. But it can be counter-productive in maintaining pursuit of that goal. Over time, merely visualising the long-term goal becomes a poor thing to rely on to generate the actions required to achieve our big goals. We need to set goals with intention and count what matters to fine tune our own money compass.

Pause and reflect:

1. *To make the invisible savings more visible, talk to your friends and family about how much money they save.*
2. *Focus your attention on your financial goals to make it less effortful to move towards them.*
3. *Go somewhere with a panoramic view to gain a fresh perspective on your big picture financial goals.*
4. *Create experiences that help you connect with your future self, e.g. talk to your parents, relatives and older people about retirement planning.*
5. *Envision your dreams to ignite excitement for the start of goal pursuit.*

Mindset 5. Setting goals with intention

Rodri's goal was to travel to 15 countries in two years. His first stop was Singapore. The country is often described as a soft landing into Asian culture. At this junction, many travellers make a decision whether to go further into experiencing Asia in all its eclectic energy and diversity. Rodri had his goal in sight and was more than ready for the adventure. In the next three months he travelled to Malaysia, Philippines, Thailand, Cambodia and Vietnam. He travelled to twelve countries in six months and was well on his way to achieving this goal.

Then a former rugby coach from high school, who had relocated to New Zealand, offered to host Rodri for three months on a workaway. The free stay was in exchange for picking blueberries at their family farm. Being a true *Lord of the Rings* fan growing up, Rodri jumped at this opportunity to experience the natural beauty in the country. Soon he landed in the South Island of New Zealand and was awe-struck with the rugged landscape. He enjoyed his stay at the farmhouse and the company from back home.

Rodri worked hard. He picked berries in the daytime and got a part-time job at a box cutting factory for an evening shift. After a few months, he saved enough money to buy a van. Over the next month, he planned to drive from the bottom of the South

Island to the top of the North Island. Barely two days into his journey, the coronavirus pandemic broke out and all plans were shelved. Rodri needed to find a temporary house and prepare for what became one of the strictest lockdowns in the world. It was during this time that Rodri was forced to reassess his travel goal. He reflected on why he wanted to travel around the world to begin with. He began to gain clarity on the situation. Past patterns of doing physical work to pay for the bills had resurfaced in his life.

He soon realised the reason why he started to travel in the first place was to find his ikigai: life purpose. In his mind's eye, he was going to become a guardian of the planet and he needed to find out where and how. He aspired to leave the places he had visited in a better state for future generations. It was at a temporary house, seeking refuge during the lockdown, where he met his soon to become life partner. He confided in her: "I don't need to travel to every corner of the world or make a million dollars. All I want is a stable and secure life with you". One month later, he got a job as a researcher in an environmental consultancy. He found this was where we could thrive as a protector, influencing policy and social change, at a larger scale. He reset his goals, fell in love and discovered his life purpose.

In the second part of Rodri's money compass, he began recalibrating his destination with a clearer vision and more deliberate intention.

$$$

Setting a fixed goal like losing 20 kilos in 6 months can be motivating, but it requires lots of hard work to maintain. Some reality TV programmes have demonstrated that these concrete goals are possible to achieve. In the show 'The Biggest Loser', participants had lost more than 20 kilos during their time on the programme. A few contestants lost more than 90 kilos. These are real significant changes, and it is truly remarkable that they are possible to achieve. Unfortunately for participants of this show, and many others trying to lose a few pounds, weight rebound is all too real. Some participants in the TV show ended up with more weight than before the programme started. One of the most replicable results in weight loss studies is the tendency for people to regain their original weight.

In one experiment, psychologist Kentaro Fujita assigned participants to two mindsets.[1] They primed participants to think of their goal either with more intention or more concretely. Some were asked a series of 'why' questions. Others were asked a series of 'how' questions. For example, participants in the first group were asked: "why would you like to maintain good physical health?" Participants in the second group were asked: "how would you like to maintain good physical health? Those who answered a series of 'why' questions were more motivated to channel time, energy and resources towards their goals. They worked harder to achieve their goals. Setting goals with intention can make all the difference.

This doesn't mean that our goals should become vague. Optimal goals describe a higher purpose with a clear set of actions. When there are no actions linked to the goal, it can turn into fantasy. And fantasy, we know, is far from reality.

$$$

"A goal properly set is halfway reached." — *Zig Ziglar*

We need to be intentional with our financial goals as well. Our broad abstract plan needs to be broken down into smaller action steps. Breaking down the big picture can transform a near impossible goal, like buying a house or saving a lump sum for retirement, into something that is possible to achieve. We are more inclined to save money if the saving amount is framed in smaller increments. One way to set our savings goal is to break things into smaller bite-sized chunks, e.g. saving $5 a day versus saving $150 a month.

In a study with a fintech company, researchers tried to get investors to commit to an automatic savings plan.[2] They framed the plan either as $150 a month, $35 a week, or $5 a day. All these amount to the same chunk of money. Among thousands of new investors using the app, they found that framing savings into daily amounts compared to monthly amounts, quadruples the number of consumers who enrol in automatic savings.

This insight of setting up smaller bite-sized goals is even more relevant when we think about saving for retirement. It can be really daunting to think about getting from where we are to this big number. Say, for example, we have a goal to save $500,000 for retirement. Psychologically, we may not be used to dealing with such large financial amounts. This may sound like a lot of money for a lot of us. But it's needed if we are going to be out of active employment for 20 to 30 years. In this time period, we may have increased medical costs and other emergency expenses.

The most we may have spent at one-go in our lifetime is a $100,000 down payment for a house or $40,000 on an electric vehicle. So when we reach $250,000 we assume that we are doing really well with our savings and dial it down. This is what has been referred to as the 'illusion of wealth'. When we translate those lump sums later in life, that's when we realise that the lump sum doesn't really add up to as much as we hoped it would. Breaking it down year by year, month by month, it's not a ton of money.

We ought to reset our big savings goal into smaller bite-sized amounts. They are easier to achieve and can be a better indicator of how much we really need.

$$$

How do we motivate ourselves when we have a clear goal?

Researchers looked at almost 10 million marathon runners and their completion times.[3] When they looked at the distribution of timings, they noticed something very odd. Many runners complete the marathon in exactly 3 hours and 59 minutes.

Finishing the race in less than 4 hours is a common goal for marathon runners. As runners get closer to the finish, realising they have a good chance of reaching this goal, they push harder and faster. This phenomenon is what is called: *the reference point* in behavioural economics. The mere act of setting a goal for ourselves creates a baseline of what 'good' looks like. It influences our behaviour and the steps we take to reach our goals.

Sometimes the reference point is set by someone else. Take the example of air mile reward programs. Studies show that people tend to take more flights with the same airline as they get closer to gaining the top status in the airline. But once people reach this goal, they take fewer flights with the same airline. After we reach a target, it feels like we've become partially reset. To overcome this reset, we need to carefully consider what types of goals we set for ourselves.

$$$

Anti-goals vs do-goals

Rodri uses anti-goals, also known as 'do-not goals', when it comes to choosing a restaurant to eat out. Anti-goals refer to the motivation to avoid something rather than achieve something. Instead of seeking vegan options, Rodri looks for places where he can easily avoid meat and dairy. This strategy has been effective for him, and he has been successful in limiting his meat and dairy consumption for over five years. It's useful in situations where we already have a strong motivation to avoid a certain behaviour. However, there is conflicting evidence that shows that the more determined we are to avoid something, the more we may obsess over it.

According to Ayelet Fishbach, who is a leading researcher in the science of motivation: the effectiveness of goal setting depends on the person and the situation. Some people and situations may benefit from setting do-goals, while others may benefit from anti-goals. In situations where the focus is on gaining or achieving something, do-goals are more appropriate than anti-goals. For instance, in dating, it makes more sense to set do-goals like 'search for romance' rather than anti-goals like 'avoid rejection'. On the other hand, anti-goals are more effective in situations where the focus is on preventing harm or escaping danger. For example, 'avoiding sunburn' can be more motivating than the goal of maintaining 'healthy skin'.

Ultimately, the most effective type of goal setting depends on the individual's personality and their situation. For Rodri's personality, anti-goals have been effective in helping him avoid meat and spending money on takeaway coffee. On the other hand, do-goals have helped him find a romantic partner and put money aside every week to reach his savings goal.

$$$

Rodri experienced how a commitment to a partner can be both irrational and effective to reach his higher-purpose life goals. This lesson was reflected to him in a research paper he came across on financial goal setting.

Dean Karlan, a Professor of Economics at Kellogg School of Management, conducted an experiment to help people with a goal to save more money.[4] Participants were assigned to either a standard savings account or a commitment account, which had the same interest rate but came with restrictions. People who selected the commitment account were required to set a savings goal or a fixed date before they could withdraw their money. Why would anyone select the commitment account? Despite the restrictions, around 30% of customers opted for the commitment account. Those who had access to the commitment account saved 80% more than those who were not offered this option. This shows how committing to a goal and introducing friction to break the commitment can be an effective way to save more money.

With the results of this experiment fresh in his mind, Rodri realised that he could apply this insight to his own life. He decided to take action and set up his own commitment account. He committed to saving $5000 in 6 months and locked himself in, knowing that he couldn't touch the money until he reached his goal. This gave him the motivation to cut back on his expenses and find ways to save money. He stopped eating out, cancelled a few online subscriptions, and found cheaper alternatives to Netflix. He was determined to make his dream of travelling the world a reality, and the commitment account was the key to achieving it.

As the months went by, Rodri watched his savings account grow, and he felt a sense of pride and accomplishment. He knew that he had made the right decision to set up the commitment account. Finally, the day arrived when he hit his savings goal. It was a moment of triumph, and Rodri felt like he had achieved something significant. This experience taught Rodri that by rerouting his money compass and committing to the destination, he could achieve anything he set his mind to. A long-term commitment to a partner was also within his capacity.

$$$

One of the countries Rodri wants to travel to next is Kenya. This is where Professor Dan Ariely and a team of researchers at Duke University have been engaged in financial experiments involving commitments.

In one study, researchers from Duke University ran an experiment to try and find new ways to increase savings.[5] They tried many clever strategies like a weekly text message reminder from the participants' kids. They matched savings with a 10% or 20% bonus every week. But the most effective solution was an expected one: a gold coin. The coin did not have any value on its own, but it reminded participants of their commitment to become a saver. Also, this coin had 24 numbers written on it that they designed. Participants were requested to put the coin somewhere safe in their house. For the next 24 weeks, they were asked to take out the coin, grab a knife and scratch the number for that week. If they reached their saving goal for the week, they scratched this number on the coin. The act of committing to and tracking goals resulted in savings that were roughly double those of the control group. Compared to offering a monetary bonus for saving, this approach proved significantly more effective.

The idea emerging from this suggests that we can influence our future behaviours with commitments and thereby reduce their likelihood of impulsive actions. When we are ready with our higher purpose goals, we can easily commit to take the actions needed to achieve them.

Yet, the process of achieving our goals can sometimes feel like a chore. By setting more intentional goals, we can reach goals that start as distant dreams. This is why it's better to set our goal as 'owning a house' rather than 'saving for a down payment'. Recognising the purpose behind our goals and setting up an action plan to achieve them is the ideal propeller to drive us towards our financial goals.

Pause and reflect:

1. *What is the underlying motivation behind achieving your financial goals?*
2. *To reach your bigger financial goals, set up small bite-sized goals with create a clear action plan, e.g. transfer $20 every week to your savings account.*
3. *Who are the people in your life that may serve as reference points for the financial milestones you wish to achieve?*
4. *Consider the situation and your personality when you are*

deciding whether to set anti-goals or do-goals.

5. *Make a public or private commitment to motivate yourself to stick with your financial goals, e.g. share your journey with your spouse, best friend or social network.*

Mindset 6. Counting what matters

Rodri made plans to meet friends from the effective altruism community for dinner. The community members alternate who picks the restaurant and this month was Rodri's turn. He picked a new plant-based pizzeria which was located in the central business district.

Since there were four others travelling from his suburb, Rodri offered to pick them up in his van. Rodri recalled, "One person in our group crunched the numbers and found that carpooling with three or more people was not only a more cost-effective option, but also the more environmentally friendly choice." This was among the topics the community group discussed at the table which included conversations on which charities to donate to and risks of artificial intelligence. Rodri ordered a sourdough pizza which cost under twenty dollars. It came with charred eggplant, pomodoro sauce and cashew mozzarella. It was the best vegan cheese he ever tasted, and the Neapolitan-style dough was near perfection. He ordered some home-brewed kombucha which cost five dollars. At this moment, they all agreed the entire dining experience was outstanding.

When the time came to leave, Rodri realised he needed to pay another twenty dollars for parking. He assumed that parking at the restaurant was complimentary. No one likes to pay for parking, especially as a surprise fee. His friends agreed to split the additional fees for parking four-ways.

Even though they would have been completely happy paying five more dollars for their pizza, it seemed like a fine to unexpectedly pay for parking. This psychological dilemma seemed to puzzle his friends. Rodri reflected, "It's because parking was only our means to get to the restaurant, but not the end goal!"

$$$

Is it a fee or is it a fine? Mr. Psychology of Money, Morgan Housel dives into the difference between the two concepts with a clear perspective.[1]

Fees are what people pay to get admission to a destination that is worthwhile going to. For example, tickets to Disneyland cost a hundred dollars. People get an amazing unforgettable day with their kids. Very few people experience this payment as a fine.

Fines are usually experienced as a punishment for doing something wrong. They often take people by surprise. Very few people are comfortable with losing 20% of their money because of factors outside their control, such as market fluctuations. The reason that it hurts many of us is because we experience the impact on our investment as an unexpected fine. We may then second guess whether we picked the wrong strategy or investment goal.

It may sound like a trivial difference. But thinking of volatility as a fee, instead of a fine, can make a big difference. This mindset shift can help us stick with our investment goals long enough to reap the benefits of compound growth. Volatility is like the unexpected parking fees. It's a fee worth paying for a destination that we may wish to get to.

$$$

Let's play a game!

In real life, most goals are too big, too small or just plain boring. An ordinary goal can be turned into a game when we self-impose an obstacle. But if we take an Uber to complete a marathon then we are not playing the game. Bernard Suits, Professor of Philosophy at the University of Waterloo, defines gameplay as: "the voluntary attempt to overcome unnecessary obstacles."[2]

Games can be manicured to design a goal that is worth pursuing. They allow us to tweak the constraints to maximise our motivation. The journey of a struggle with the internal agency to achieve something can yield immense satisfaction. As the idea of bounded rationality has it, we don't have the cognitive resources to evaluate all our life decisions. But in a game, we have clarity of values. We all agree on a simple point system. There is a certain 'cognitive yumminess' that draws us towards numbers that we all hold to be true.[3] This is the point where things get dangerously seductive.

Conspiracies often tap into this innate desire for sense-making with numbers. They offer us a simplified explanation of the world. As you climb up the ranks of Scientology, there's an achievement that can be unlocked called 'going clear'. It is considered the highest level of spiritual attainment you can reach. But this application of points is not just limited to conspiracy theorists.

The concept of gamification is widely adopted by many technology companies. Completing 10,000 steps with our Fitbit tracker is a goal that is preset for many people. Interestingly, people get more motivated to complete a goal as they get closer to reaching it. A prominent behavioural scientist admitted, "Even I pace up and down my bedroom at night just to hit my 10,000-step goal on my fitness tracker."

Tread carefully when simplifying life goals into numbers. As discussed in the previous story, many marathon runners cross the finish line in exactly 3 hours and 59 minutes. Setting financial goals with a clear number can be the motivation we need to move towards our goals. But we must be careful when it comes to making sense of what these numbers mean and what they don't mean.

$$$

For our investment decisions, what really counts are the decisions we make on a small number of days when everyone around us is going into a frenzy. If we continue to invest one dollar in the stock market every month, rain or shine, we will perform much better than someone who sells during a recession.

But for our financial goals, counting what matters is not easy. We can turn to Ayelet Fishbach, Professor of Behavioral Science at the University of Chicago, for five tips on counting our goals.[4]

Tip 1. Easy to measure targets

Consider the following examples for counting a reading goal:
I will read 30,000 characters a day
I will read 6,000 words a day
I will read 20 pages a day

While they are all approximately the same target, we have a hard time evaluating whether we completed reading 30,000 characters or 6,000 words because counting characters and words is exhausting. 20 pages a day is far easier to track.

When setting our savings or investment goals, we need to consider whether it is easy enough for us to measure. If we make it easy to do, we are more likely to count it!

Tip 2. Action-oriented targets

What if the price of empty calories are more action-oriented? Imagine a world in which food calories are labelled in terms of exercise required. Food quantity is counted by the number of steps or other forms of physical activity needed to take to burn it off. A compelling study showed teenagers reduced their soda purchases when they found out that they will need to jog 50 minutes to burn off the extra calories.[5]

Action-oriented targets are simply intuitively meaningful targets. We already set them up for ourselves. Some examples include brushing your teeth twice daily, calling parents once a week and reading for twenty minutes a day before bed.

The metrics that we currently use to measure our progress on financial goals need to specify what steps we need to take to get there. This can be as simple as making sure that we transfer 50 dollars to our savings account before the end of the month.

Tip 3. Self-set targets

One risk of allowing others to set our targets is that we might feel the urge to rebel. This is what psychologists call 'psychological reactance'. When other people set our goals, we may find ourselves reverting to past patterns. It could remind us of a time when we did not have agency to make our own decisions.

When it comes to our money matters, things are personal. Requests to change our financial behaviours may feel like a threat to our sense of agency and autonomy. For some of us, cancelling a Netflix subscription can cause more financial damage than good. We may end up spending Friday night out instead of a quiet night home watching a documentary with friends. It could be a source of comfort if we are living alone or a source of inspiration to become a better home chef.

Tip 4. Malicious targets

This is a story that Professor Ayelet Fishbach narrates from Hanoi in the early 1900s.

The fancy new sewer system in the former French colony enabled rats to thrive. It was only recently that scientists discovered rats were responsible for the last plague. To tackle this problem, the French colonists created a bounty programme. They incentivised locals with one cent for every rat killed. It seemed to go well. Within a month tens of thousands of rats were killed every day. Then, to the surprise of health officials, mutated rats without tails were spotted all around the city.

Rat hunters were only required to provide the tails as proof of work. Soon the unintended consequence of this policy became known to health officials. As nature has it, you need rats to breed more rats. Local bounty hunters caught rats and set them back to the sewer system to allow them to breed. A classic perverse incentive rewarding people to make the issue worse. Some enterprising hunters even developed farming operations for large-scale breeding. In the end, the incentive programme tragically failed, with more, not fewer rats roaming the streets in Vietnam.

Clearly, counting people's actions can modify behaviour. But if we count the wrong thing, we promote the wrong behaviours.

Tip 5. Self-compassionate targets

Remember the "get out of jail card" from the previous story? Participants who had emergency reserves were more likely to persist with their goals, despite a minor failure. In the context of self-compassionate targets, this means setting goals with a certain level of flexibility can help us move towards our intended destination. By allowing some slack when we stray, it makes us more likely to stick with our goals.

If we are experiencing a financially challenging time, that's okay. There are many unforeseen circumstances that we may encounter in our lifetime. Financial goals and targets can feel out of bounds. This is almost inevitable for most of us. At these times, we can focus our attention on self-care and wellbeing practices. This builds our long-term capacity to tackle financial goals when we are in a position to do so. We've got this!

Pause and reflect:

1. *If your savings or investment is unexpectedly impacted, re-frame this as a fee that is worth paying to reach your long-term goals.*
2. *Set your financial goal with a number to motivate yourself, but periodically evaluate whether this number is helpful.*
3. *Adopt the five tips for counting goals: (1) Create easy-to-*

measure targets, (2) Design action-oriented targets, (3) Self-set your own targets, (4) Avoid malicious targets, and (5) Allow slack with self-compassionate targets.

III

Stories of Kaya

Kaya resets her money thermostat

On a cold winter day, Kaya wrote an article about her money thermostat. Just like a thermostat regulates the temperature in a room, habits play a crucial role in regulating how she handles her money. Kaya explained, "In the past, I've noticed that when my bank balance exceeds a baseline, I tend to automatically spend more money without thinking twice. But, when my bank balance falls below that baseline, I find clever ways to cut back on unwanted expenses and save money. It's as if my money thermostat is programmed to revert to the baseline bank balance." Essentially, money habits are to bank balances what thermostats are to room temperature.

Kaya recalled the instance when she overcame her habit of unhealthy snacking at night. First, she tried to break the habit with sheer willpower and determination. Despite being regarded as a strong personality by many, the willpower strategy simply wasn't working for her. As an avid reader, she read many books on the science of habits which prompted her to examine the context, routines and rewards of her money thermostat. She noted that her snacking mostly took place at night, typically a post work treat, and usually while watching TV in the living room. She decided to change the baseline in her money thermostat by removing all unhealthy snacks from her living room. She reset the environment with healthier snacks like dark chocolate, almonds and pumpkin seeds to claim her post work reward.

By resetting her money thermostat, Kaya was able to break her unhealthy nighttime snacking routine and turned it into a routine of healthy food. In this story, we explore the three mindsets that Kaya adopted in the context of money habits. We reflect on how these mindsets can help us change the baseline of our own money thermostat.

Mindset 7. Context creates the habit

Kaya's favourite jazz ensemble is performing in her local city. The tickets are expensive, but she's dreamed of seeing this group perform live for many years. She says to herself: "This will be worth every penny and more". Kaya cut down some regular monthly expenses so she could spend a little more on front row seats.

That same week her television broke down. There's no way she could've predicted this ill-fated event. There are few budget options available. But since she replaces this gadget only once every five years, she doesn't want an outdated model. Kaya decides to bite the bullet and pay extra for the latest 8K screen smart TV.

Next week marks her ten-year wedding anniversary. She hasn't ever celebrated anniversaries, but this year she wants to celebrate the occasion. Ten years with her partner marks a landmark occasion. Kaya decides to splurge on an extravagant surprise party with a live band, catered gourmet food and a cocktail bar.

There is some missing context behind Kaya's spending spree. She decided to spend extra on the front row seats because a pop-up notification offered a 50% discounted price for the upgrade. When she went to the electronics store to buy a budget replacement, the salesperson played into her fears of purchasing an obsolete TV. Three weeks before her wedding anniversary, her best friend celebrated a housewarming with catered food and drinks. Kaya's partner couldn't stop raving about the party. She wanted to pull out all the stops to please her partner.

Context creates the habit. Without the context, Kaya's spending habits may seem like a self-control issue. Taking the context into account, we can see a clearer pattern. Poignant aspects in her physical and social environment spurred her on this spree.

$$\$\$\$$$

This thought experiment on unplanned expenses is from a paper titled *The exception is the rule.*[1] The central idea is that one-off expenses can come up rather frequently in our lives. We may not know what this expense will be. But what we can learn from Kaya's spending habits is that there will always be a one-off expense. Be it the inevitable replacement for the car tyre or unexpected medical treatment when travelling to a foreign country without travel insurance.

We have a strange, yet beautiful human trait that psychologists refer to as *the introspection illusion*. It gives us confidence and other essential ingredients, such as dopamine and motivation, to meet life's challenges head on. However, it also leads us to overlook the powerful influences from the physical and social world that are outside our control. We are constantly immersed in our environment and influenced by others. We may pretend that self-control shapes our habits. But this delusion ignores the fact that our nervous system is always running like mobile phone apps that continue to run in the background.

Humans explore and exploit. Our exploration involves gathering information, and our exploitation involves using this information to get a predictable and secure outcome.[2] For example, the first few times we feel stressed, we may seek strategies that help us feel calm and settled. We may discover that movement is a useful outlet to help us relax as the adrenaline channels through the body instead of remaining fixed, causing inflammation. We may find out that caffeine triggers more anxiety in this state so we may avoid it. The nervous system catalogues our explorations. This is the driving force behind all our habits. Essentially, habits are reliable responses to recurring conditions in our context.

$$$

What happens if the context is forever changing?

For the airline industry, spending money on one-off expenses ends up occurring at high frequency. Hurricane Katrina, mechanic strikes, ground staff shortages, fuel price shocks and other non-recurring expenses happen with a fair amount of regularity. When risk analysts are asked: "Is there going to be a one-off expense for the airline due to a natural disaster next year?" This answer is typically categorised as very unlikely. But if the question posed is: "Is there going to be a one-off expense of the same size next year?" The answer is categorised as very likely.[3]

This sort of reframing made analysts at an airline company question their own forecasts and better prepare the company's forecasts for unexpected events. Behavioural economists use the term 'mental accounting' to describe how we learn to categorise money saving and spending.

It is easier to mentally allocate a budget for recurring expenses like rent, food, mobile phones, and Netflix subscriptions since they are predictable and incurred monthly. On the other hand, we never know when an unexpected expense may arise. Our learning model excludes them from our mental accounts of expenses. We learn that one-time expenses should be dismissed. They happen just once after all, so they don't need a separate category to be remembered.

Unfortunately, we tend to neglect one key aspect in all this. While each one-off expense is unpredictable, the category of 'unexpected expenses' is fairly predictable and sometimes rather frequent. Even though the particular one-time expense of replacing a broken TV might not happen for another five years, another unplanned expense inevitably crops up soon after.

Understandably, this means that covering unexpected expenses is the most common reason for withdrawal from retirement accounts. We may believe that these are one-off expenses, so they don't matter for our planning. In a Pew research study, 60% of households report having an unplanned financial shock in the last 12 months and 55% of households struggled to 'make ends meet' after their most expensive unpredictable expense.[4]

From a motivational perspective, many of us have a habit of spending more on one-off expenses too. Splurging on a one-time expense is easy to justify, simply by thinking that it's not likely to happen again. We may tell ourselves, on this occasion, we ought to spend more than we normally would. So we forget the frequency of each one-off expense.

Are we likely to have a one-time expense come up soon? Chances are it's more likely than we think. We ought to consider how we can account for this and make a back-up plan so that our own budgets are prepared for the unexpected.

$$$

What happened in the swimming pool at the Beijing 2008 Olympics was extraordinary. No swimmer had ever defended a butterfly title in the Olympics. But Michael Phelps is unlike any other swimmer. He was expected to defend his title and comfortably win. After all, he is known as the king of the butterfly stroke. His technique is absolutely flawless.

After three consecutive gold medals in Beijing, Michael Phelps was on the brink of success in this crucial race. It would cement his place in Olympic history as the most decorated gold medalist of all time. But soon after he dived into the pool, his goggles broke and filled with water. He needed to swim the remaining 130 metres of the race blind. His coach Bob Bowman recalled: "I thought he was either really tired or he was getting sick. Because I could tell he wasn't moving." His coach, like the rest of the world, expected Phelps to blaze past the other swimmers. He was struggling and the race was now wide open for anyone to win.

Michael Phelps had trained for unexpected situations. Coach Bob Bowman would invent new ways to put the celebrity athlete outside his comfort zone. He even once cracked his $200 goggles before a race just to train him. This exposure in practice sessions prepared Phelps to confront situations under pressure.

Fast forward to the 2008 Beijing Olympics — Men's 200 metre butterfly. Michael Phelps was prepared for water to enter his goggles. He started to count the number of strokes with an internal rhythm built over years of training. He executed this back-up plan and went on to win this race. Today, with twenty-three Olympic gold medals to his name, Michael Phelps is the most decorated Olympian of all time.

One of the key lessons we can draw from this story is to aim for the best while preparing for the unexpected.

$$$

Kaya is no newcomer when it comes to back-up plans. She surgically conducts a 'pre-mortem' for all things that can possibly go wrong with her projects at work. Now, she has adopted this strategy of expecting the unexpected for managing her personal finance too.

From experience, Kaya knows there's always a chance that things will fall through at the last minute. Say, for example, Michael Phelps is the preferred athlete to cast in an advertising campaign for a client. Even after the deal is confirmed, she expects the unexpected. There are many potential scenarios that can still break the deal. Remember when Michael Phelps was suspended by USA Swimming after being arrested for driving under the influence? For the brand, this is one of many possible deal-breakers.

Obstacles are an inevitable part of planning in the advertising industry. Here's how Kaya plans for the unexpected. First, she creates a list of all the things that might go wrong in her project. This is followed with a thorough back-up plan for potential obstacles that she may encounter. She commissions extensive research to identify suitable influencers that match the brand. This is based on who represents the brand's promise and who the target audience will best relate to. She then narrows the scope down to three names. If need be, she has the list of other celebrities ready to pursue at her fingertips.

The strategy applies to anyone involved in managing large-scale projects. Product managers have stories of the mobile app crashing minutes before the big launch. Team leaders often lose key employees in the middle of a massive project. Budgets are often slashed during an ongoing project. A good planner like Kaya performs a pre-mortem for unexpected events. This means having a back-up plan at her disposal before the catastrophic event even occurs.

It takes up a considerable amount of cognitive resource to make a back-up plan when in crisis mode. The pre-mortem allows us to adopt a more flexible approach. This can help us reorient ourselves in the midst of calamity. What is our plan B, plan C and plan D? We may need to pivot strategy rapidly when we encounter a new obstacle. It's crucial to have alternatives in the back pocket.

They say "predictions are for chimps." A once in a hundred-year pandemic may be impossible to predict. More often than not, the exact nature of the calamity is impossible to predict. However, the act of preparing for obstacles trains our neural circuitry to anticipate a wide range of possibilities. In this practice, we are resetting the baseline for our money thermostat too.

$$$

In isolation, there are no good and bad habits. All habits are simply learned responses that we've catalogued as something that is useful. Habits serve some underlying purpose in our lives. Good habits are the responses that move us towards our long-term goals while bad habits push us further away from these goals.

For example, let's consider Kaya's habit of binge-watching TV shows on Netflix. It helps her unwind after a long day of work.

Often, the next episode starts without having to move a muscle. She doesn't have to make a conscious decision. It's designed to be incredibly friction-less for her to keep watching the TV show. But this means that she gives up sleep at night and feels miserable at work the next day. While binge-watching Netflix may have been pleasurable at the time, lack of sleep does not align with her long-term health and wellbeing goals.

The forces in this context make it easy to binge-watch. Like objects in the physical world are subject to gravity, our habits are constantly subject to internal and external forces. Some of the internal forces are our goals, feelings and mental models. The context also generates external forces on our habits. This is everything in the world surrounding us. It includes the location we are in, people we are with and their attitudes and emotional states, time of day and our past actions.

A natural experiment in the United States revealed that 9 out of 10 states with the lowest smoking rates are places where smoking is prohibited in workplaces, restaurants and bars. According to leading habit expert Professor Wendy Wood, around 40% of people's daily activities are performed each day in almost the same context.[5] In the case of smoking, people now have to exit the office building or leave their drink at the pub to go smoking. Changing the environment adds friction which makes the behaviour less likely to occur.

Restraining forces can be thought of as friction that impedes certain actions. When we hit the brakes, we are relying on friction. There are restraining forces like tobacco control laws that increase the friction on smoking. Other social forces, such as seeing fewer people smoke around us can shift our behaviour.

Context is the petri dish from which our habits emerge. There are plenty of self-experiments that we can run to add friction or remove friction. These are the forces that make our good habits and bad habits.

$$\$\$\$$$

How does moving money from one bank account to another account labelled 'holiday savings' help people save money? Rationally, all economists know a dollar is a dollar. There is a theory in economics that illustrates that money is fungible. It shouldn't matter where we got the dollar or how we store the dollar. It should all be treated the same. But we also know that money in a 'holiday savings' account can add the friction that we need to stay on track for our long-term goals.

A more realistic view of how we treat money is evident in our tendency to place money in different buckets. Bucketing, or to be more formal: mental accounting, is part of our human nature to categorise information. For example, when we think of the category of a bird, we know that they have wings and fly. So when we come across a bird in the future, we can reasonably guess what behaviours to expect.[3] In the context of finances, we carry out a similar categorisation with money. We account for how much we earn and spend with a salary bucket, rent bucket or savings bucket. One consequence of this is that we don't think of our salary the same as money we receive as inheritance. We might view the latter as extra, or even a treat.

Professor Katy Milkman and John Beshears found that people changed their grocery spending when they were given 10-dollar coupons at the supermarket.[6] In their experiment, people spent more than they normally would at the store. Moreover, they also bought items that they would not typically buy. This 'windfall effect' shows up even when it is our own money that is returned to us. This has been observed with tax reimbursements. People tend to spend the same reimbursement on multiple occasions. So we may end up overspending money when it is returned to us. Bizarrely, we spend our windfall many times over until we are poorer than we were before.

More money does not always create more wealth. Wealth is a factor of how we treat money from different sources. The context in which we make money, spend money and plan for unexpected expenses is what influences our wealth.

Pause and reflect:

1. *Instead of thinking of self-control, evaluate how your physical and social environment influences your habits.*
2. *You are always learning new habits that are safe and reliable responses to similar situations.*
3. *Remember that unexpected expenses, by definition, will occur more frequently than you expect.*
4. *Prepare back-up plans for all the things that may block you from achieving your financial goals, e.g. If 'X' happens, then I will do 'Y'.*
5. *Run experiments with yourself, removing friction to enable good habits and adding friction to block bad habits.*

Mindset 8. Consistency compounds

Kaya now shapes the context to change her money habits. Last week, she avoided getting her regular lunch from the cafe opposite her workplace. She started preparing the next day's lunch while making dinner. It does take some effort, but she persists with her new behaviour. Similar to what happened with her other good habits, she patiently waits for the day this becomes automatic.

Borrowing an idea from Wendy Wood's book *Good Habits, Bad Habits*, Kaya likened this to her sleeping behaviours.[1] Not when she falls asleep. Not what time she would ideally like to sleep. But when is the moment she slips into sleep? It's impossible for her to get an answer. When she tries to examine the exact moment that she falls asleep, it keeps her awake. Every night, she simply gets into bed, and after reading a few pages of a book or yarning with her partner, they switch off the light. This is sometimes followed by moments of tossing left and right. Then, she falls asleep. Next thing she knows it's 7:00am and the sun is shining.

Habit works the same way. Kaya initiates a habit like packing home-made lunch for work the next day. She repeats this task. Then one day, it happens automatically. She doesn't forget to buy ingredients to make her lunch or get tempted with outside cafeteria food. She has a nutritious home-cooked meal available when she needs it. At some point, it all becomes second nature, and she lets autopilot drive this good habit. After ten years of adopting this good habit, she notices the savings in her bank have snowballed into a small fortune. Her wealth multiplies because of the power of compounding. But it's Kaya's consistency that makes the compounding automatic.

$$$

Would you rather take $1,000,000 next month or $0.01 that doubles in value every day for 30 days?

The first option for a million dollars next month appears to be a no-brainer. Yet it seems like a trick question. To our unchecked intuition, it is difficult to fathom how one cent can multiply into the excess of five million dollars. The second option would make us more than five times richer at the end of the month.

This is the magic of compounding. The returns challenge our imagination of what is possible with our savings. One challenge we face is that linear thinking is more intuitive than exponential thinking. A small starting base can morph into a number so large that it seems too good to be true. We don't have to be extraordinary savers to become wealthy. Ordinary savings, for a consistent period of time, can generate a big pay-off.

Morgan Housel makes the case for compounding in the book *Psychology of Money.*[2] More than 2,000 books are dedicated to how Warren Buffet built his fortune. When we study how multi-billionaire Warren Buffet became rich, we tend to overlook the key drivers to his wealth. Few pay attention to the simple fact that his fortune is not down to being a good investor alone. But it is about being a good investor for a consistent period of time. With a net worth of more than $80 billion dollars, more than 95% of his fortune was accumulated after his 65th birthday. He is a phenomenal investor. But a key point is missed if we attach his investing acumen to his investment choices alone. The real story was that he was a consistent investor for 75 years.

Warren Buffet began investing when he was 10. By the time he was 30, he had a net worth of about a million dollars. Effectively all of Warren Buffet's financial success can be tied to the base he established and the habit he continued to maintain. His skill is investing—but his superpower is consistency.

$$$

"Time magnifies the margin between success and failure. It will multiply whatever you feed it. Good habits make time your ally. Bad habits make time your enemy." — James Clear

Habits are not always intuitive. It's easy to overestimate the importance of a single action. It's also easy to underestimate the impact of many small actions. A useful mental model is to think of habits as the compound interest of self-improvement.

James Clear makes the point for small continuous improvement in his book *Atomic Habits*.[3] Improving by 1% is not always noticeable. But it can be very meaningful in the long-term. Here's how the maths works out: If we can get 1% better at something each day for one year, we will get 37 times better by the end of the year. The impact a tiny improvement can have with consistency is simply astounding.

Consider how this works in the context of learning a new

language. Say, we put in a single 90-minute focussed learning session today. It may seem like we are no more fluent today than we were yesterday. We've only progressed 1% in our ability to speak this new language. But what starts as small changes, slowly and surely accumulates to a 3700% improvement. After one year, we may feel more comfortable in starting a basic conversation in a completely foreign language.

Similarly, if we avoid going out for Friday night drinks, it does not make us a millionaire tomorrow. We might dismiss small changes because they don't seem to make a significant difference in our bank balance. The results don't seem to come quickly so we slide back to previous routines. Unfortunately, the slow pace of change also makes it easy for a bad habit to creep back in. One expensive night of binge drinking with friends is simple enough to overcome. But when we repeat 1% errors, our bad habits compound into something much bigger.

Making a choice that is 1% better seems insignificant in the present moment. Yet the continuous impact is profound. It is only when looking back, say ten years later, that the value of good habits becomes strikingly apparent. They may seem to make little difference on reaching our financial goals. But in the span of moments—which meld to form a lifetime—these choices have a major impact on making or breaking our dreams.

Clearly, we should be more concerned with our habits than our current financial situation. If someone is a millionaire, but they have a habit of spending more than they earn, they are on a negative trajectory. When spending habits exceed saving habits, the good times are not going to last very long. On the flip side, if we don't have much at the moment but save a little every month then we are on the path toward securing a better financial future.

$$$

One of the virtues for us to grow our good habits is *grit*. An-gela Duckworth, Professor of Psychology at the University of Pennsylvania popularised this idea.[4] As a behavioural scientist, she made it her personal mission to evaluate what it takes to become successful in any field. She conducted interviews with corporate salespeople, successful athletes, and elite military training graduates to figure out what made them successful.

There were two major factors that contributed to their success. These factors were not good looks, physical health, intellectual potential or even social intelligence—it was grit. Grit is a psychological concept that refers to the combination of perseverance and passion for a well defined long-term goal. It is the ability to work hard for this goal, and maintain focus and determination, even in the face of setbacks or obstacles. Angela Duckworth's work showcases that success is not determined by talent, but rather by a person's grit

Will Smith is often cited as an example of someone who embodies the concept of grit. He has achieved success in a variety of fields including acting, music, and producing. He is known for his relentless work ethic and dedication to his craft, as well as his ability to bounce back from setbacks and continue to pursue his goals.

In a now famous interview, he shared that he never viewed himself as more talented than others. He admitted that what really set him apart from others was down to his work ethic. That's what made him famous. He went on to say: "You might have more talent than me, you might be smarter than me, you might be sexier than me, you might be all of those things, you got it on me in nine categories. But if we get on the treadmill together, there's two things: You're getting off first, or I'm going to die."

Now, that's the flip side of this virtue called grit.

"The opposite of a great virtue is also a great virtue" — Phil Tetlock (author of Superforecasting)

Do we really want to push ourselves to the point of burnout? In some cases, quitting is a virtue and also a moral imperative. Consider a startup employing 150 people that is close to bankruptcy and the writing is on the wall. Fairytale stories of people who have miraculously turned things around against all odds and go on to make a fortune do exist. But they are the exception, not the rule. Is the founder CEO really doing the right thing by pretending all is well? Do the employees deserve to know about the financial situation so they can start searching for other opportunities if or when the need arises?

The virtue of quitting is explored by Annie Duke in her book *Quit*.[5] Duke, a former top-flight poker player, maintains that the biggest mistake rookies make is playing too many hands and not knowing when to quit. She argues that there is a time for grit and a time to quit.

Climbing Mount Everest is a test of strength, endurance, and determination. It's a gruelling challenge that requires grit and perseverance. But what happens when the situation calls for quitting? Many mountaineers refuse to quit and have lost their lives as a result.

She references the story from Jon Krakauer's book *Into Thin Air* about three climbers who were three hundred yards from the top of Mount Everest. Dr. Stuart Hutchinson, John Taske, and Lou Kasischke, who were part of a climbing expedition in the 1990s. On Summit Day, the climbers set out to reach the top of the world. But as they climbed, they encountered traffic jams and it was slow going. When their expedition leader passed them and estimated it would take them three more hours to reach the summit, they realised they wouldn't make it before the turnaround time.

Hutchinson convinced the group to turn around and head back down the mountain because they were well past the cut-off time. It was a decision that saved their lives. The southeast ridge, the path they would have had to descend in darkness, is a narrow and dangerous route. Falling would have meant certain death. They followed the cut-off time, and made the 'boring' decision to quit. They showed us that knowing when to quit can be just as important as knowing when to push on.

Quitting is often seen as a negative thing, yet in this case, it was a smart decision. It's courageous to have grit but it's equally heroic to know when to quit. Because sometimes quitting is the morally right thing to do. It takes humility and wisdom to walk away to safeguard our survival. If we survive for long enough, we will thrive with the power of compounding.

$$$

How long does it take to form a new habit?

Rumour has it that it takes 21 days of repetition to form a new habit. This 21-day myth can be traced to a 1960s self-help book by a cosmetic surgeon titled *Psycho Cybernetics*. The answer is not this straightforward as explained by Professor of Psychology and habits expert, Wendy Wood.

The real magic begins silently and we won't know the exact moment it kicks in. Like falling asleep, we just need to trust it will happen. It is the standard way in which repeated actions rewires our neural pathways to support humans to learn new behaviours. Until we have laid down a habit in our neural networks and memory systems, we must intentionally set our goals and repeat this action again and again. It requires constant effort.

In one experiment, 96 students were paid 40 dollars each in a 3-month-long study.[6] The aim was to test how long it would take to form a new habit. Each participant named a healthy behaviour that they were not yet doing but they wanted to perform regularly. At the end of each day, participants reported whether they performed the habit as planned and to what extent the new behaviour was automatic.

At the beginning of the study, the new habits were low on the automatic rating (3 out of 42 points). They were learning new behaviours like eating healthily or exercising frequently and it did not feel automatic. When the action is hardest to do, our habit memory is doing the most learning. The more participants repeated a behaviour, the more automatic it became.

Reassuringly for many of us, participants were able to pick up a habit even after missing a day or two. Occasional gaps did not erase an emerging habit. This is a crucial point. Habits are not so rigid that they need perfection. They require persistence, repetition and setting a context that can make a big difference. Think of it like the 'good enough' approach to parenting. Parents don't have to be perfect all the time to form secure attachments with their child. They just need to be good enough, most of the time.

On average, it took participants about 66 days to cement their new habits. There was some variation, however; healthier eating took about 65 days to become a habit. Exercise required 91 days. It makes sense that some habits involving simple behaviours become habits quicker than ones that require more effort. A key takeaway from this experiment is that there is no script for how long it will take to form a new habit. Depending on the type of habit, different people will take different amounts of time. The bottom line is consistent: new habits become easier and more automatic with repetitions.

Knowledge is a lagging measure of our good reading habits. Clutter is a lagging measure of our bad cleaning habits. Our net worth is a lagging measure of our money habits. We get what we repeat—consistency compounds!

Pause and reflect:

1. *Your good habits will become easy and automatic with repetition.*
2. *Ordinary savings for a consistent period of time will generate extraordinary returns*
3. *Time will multiply small changes to your saving or spending habits.*
4. *Your success will be determined by grit, but it's also helpful to quit what does not serve you.*
5. *Your good habits don't have to be perfect, it just needs to be good enough for a long time.*

Mindset 9. Reward the small wins

The thought of spending less and saving more was out of the question for Kaya. She tried setting fixed budgets and putting her money into a savings account on the day she received her salary. But ultimately, she didn't feel rewarded in the process. She did not stick with it for a sustained period of time.

One day she stumbled upon the concept of temptation bundling in the book *How to Change.*[1] Professor Katy Milkman's examples in the book tempted her to run a small self-experiment. One habit Kaya enjoyed was watching Netflix, but the guilt of wasting time always dampened her mood. She tested this idea by bundling one 'good habit' with one so-called 'bad habit'. Every time she felt the pull to watch Netflix (this was her self-assigned bad habit), she would set five minutes aside to check her account balances (this was her self-assigned good habit).

At first, it felt like a chore to do this. But this way, she was able to enjoy watching her favourite show while also developing a habit of checking her transactions, avoiding overdraft fees and cancelling subscriptions that she no longer used. Soon, she found that by associating this bad habit with saving money, she was able to watch her favourite TV show guilt-free. After this positive experience with rewarding her good habit, she started applying this mindset for rewarding other financial goals.

She cancelled six app subscriptions on her phone that she rarely used. She realised that treating herself with an occasional avocados-on-toast brunch did not hurt her financial goals. When she reached one of her landmark saving goals, she asked her partner to pack a bag for the long weekend. They boarded a flight together to a surprise destination. She was grateful to be able to celebrate these small wins with her partner.

$$$

Have you wondered why 99% of the world's toothpaste tastes like mint?

The craving for mint becomes our cue for a reward, even before we start brushing. This is the so-called mint effect at play.[2] Before we brush, we anticipate the fresh tingly sensation of mint. When we start to brush, we register the successful engagement of a pleasant experience. After we finish brushing, our reward system makes an association. Connecting the routine of brushing our teeth with the reward of a minty toothpaste is how we make it an automatic habit.

As behavioural science aficionado Rory Sutherland highlights: "People say it's for dental health. But when you look at when people brush their teeth, first thing in the morning, certainly before they go on a date, you realise that deep down, it's much more about fear of bad breath than it is long-term dental maintenance." Rory's book *Alchemy* explored the innovation of stripe coloured toothpastes.[3] It's a classic case of the psychological innovation being more revolutionary than the technological one.

It took years of engineering to develop a toothpaste to come out perfectly as three stripes. In reality, the active ingredients were evenly spread through the entire tube so it had nothing beneficial for consumers. Then in the early 60s, marketers realised that the triple stripe technology could signal that the toothpaste had three clear benefits. People bought into the story that three stripes were evidence that this toothpaste could: (1) fight cavities, (2) tackle infections and (3) freshen the breath, all at the same time.

The precise rationale for a reward is less relevant. The triple-striped toothpaste shows that the celebration can be purely psychological. A reinforcing feedback loop that rewards a routine is what tips an action from being a new behaviour into becoming a lasting habit.

$$$

Building up an appetite.

In yoga, fasting is for controlling our major *klesha* (Sanskrit word for impurity). This can be understood as an unhealthy attachment to a particular thing. Rewards are classified as 'appetitive behaviour' in the scientific literature. They create an appetite for more of those behaviours that give us pleasure. As is true with fasting practices, our internal reward system can benefit from disruptions to motivate ourselves. One of the best things we can do to achieve our goals is to reward the completion of key milestones. But to make this effective, we need to avoid the celebration every once in a while.[4] Skipping the routine celebration fine tunes our dopamine system to complete our goals.

Here's a detailed example of how to use this strategy of 'intermittent reinforcement' for our rewards. Say, we have a savings goal that involves getting a fixed amount by a certain date. We may then break that goal down into smaller achievable milestones. If the goal is to save $10,000 in one year, the milestones might be to save $1,000 per month. This builds an emergency reserve for two months where we may fall short of the savings goal.

Once the milestone is reached, a self-reward can be unlocked, such as treating ourselves to a spa day. It is important that these rewards are not given every time a milestone is reached, but only once every now and then. This is similar to how a slot machine operates. It creates an appetite for more of those behaviours that give us pleasure and enhances our drive to persist.

The comparison with a slot machine can be seen in how it relies on intermittent reinforcement to encourage people to gamble. The rewards are never guaranteed every time the lever is pulled, only occasionally. When we avoid rewarding ourselves every time we reach a milestone, but instead only treat ourselves occasionally, it creates an appetite for more of the good habits.

$$$

1-minute dopamine schedule.

Dopamine is a chemical in the brain that is involved in our experience of rewards. It is often referred to as the 'feel good' chemical because it energises us to pursue actions that have positive consequences and meet our goals. The timing of the reward is key to how dopamine influences our behaviours.

For example, when we hear the familiar jingle of an ice cream van, the novelty and salience of the sound activates dopamine in the brain. This early stage of the dopamine response, known as salience, startles us into attention and we get a craving. The decision to buy an ice cream spikes the dopamine levels in our reward system. As we cherish our blueberry ice-cream on a hot summer day, the reward strengthens our ice-cream habit.

On the topic of timely, Kaya wishes to call out the song widely played by ice cream vans. Because, it's not okay. The song, *Turkey in the Straw* has racist origins that date back to the 19th century. It can unintentionally, and sometimes intentionally, perpetuate harmful stereotypes.

The timing of the reward is relevant since dopamine promotes learning a habit for less than 1-minute after the action. If we were to receive an unanticipated reward in the future, such as a paycheck bonus in two weeks, it would not change neural connections in the same way as a reward experienced right after our response. This is because the response to the dopamine spike immediately after the action is what builds habit associations.

$$\$\$\$$$

Intrinsic motivation refers to the internal drive to engage in a behaviour or activity for its own sake, rather than for external rewards or incentives. This type of motivation is important for achieving financial goals because it allows individuals to find personal meaning and satisfaction in the act of setting and reaching those goals, rather than relying solely on external rewards or consequences.

An example of intrinsic motivation in relation to financial goals are the feelings of accomplishment and pride that arise from setting and achieving our goals. This type of self-motivation can help us stick to our financial plans and embed them as a habit.

Another example is the warm glow of generosity that comes from volunteering or helping others. This feeling can be a powerful motivator for achieving financial wellbeing, as it can inspire individuals to prioritise their financial goals and stay connected with their community. When we form a habit of setting and achieving financial goals, the warm glow of satisfaction and accomplishment sets in, making it more likely that we will continue the habit of achieving our financial goals.

In short, intrinsic motivation can play an important role in helping individuals achieve their financial goals. This is done by providing a sense of personal fulfilment and satisfaction, and by making the act of setting and achieving goals a habit that is self-reinforcing.

$$\$\$\$$$

Behavioural scientist Dan Arieley recalls his visit to a poor township in Soweto, which is a suburb of Johannesburg.[5] The city is colloquially known as the *City of God* and is also the financial hub of South Africa. This is a city where multinationals and major South African banks have their headquarters. But many residents in this township are underserved by both government and financial services.

The author recalls when he sat in a financial establishment that sold funeral insurance. Some people he interviewed spend up to two years of their income on funeral services. At least we have only one funeral in our lifetime. Similar to big wedding celebrations, funerals are an expensive proposition in South Africa.

A father and son dropped in. The father bought himself funeral insurance for a week. This only covers him if he dies within the next seven days. Then in a very ceremonial way, he handed the piece of paper over to his son. The family may have had less food on the table that week but they are comforted in knowing their father will get a dignified funeral. The act of spending a significant portion of their weekly income on funeral insurance was a ritual. It was a celebration that was visible for all members of the family to observe.

$$$

We all know someone who is incredibly rich but extremely unhappy. An unwritten rule for happiness is to hold our expectations lightly. This is not to say that we shouldn't have dreams. In the last story, we've seen the role of goal setting to move us towards our dreams and aspirations. However, it is not helpful to hold up our expectations as a central source of joy and happiness in our lives.[6]

In an ideal scenario, we ought to have low expectations. Then our financial outcomes, both good and bad, are handled with a certain degree of stoicism. We are not as moved by these changes. Like one-time expenses and compounding, changes in our lives are constant. A level of stoicism is about acceptance of the unknown. Investing has a constant chain of surprises, volatility, setbacks, and disappointment. But if we can stick around long enough, the odds of compounding work to our advantage.

The story we tell ourselves matters. We may say: "I hope to save enough for a house deposit in the future". But when we identify happiness too closely with our expectations, we may say: "I am only happy if I will save enough for a house deposit".

For many of us, the upward swing in our fortune is more important than what we already have. We may tell ourselves the story that if we just get one pay raise, we will be so much happier. But this wasn't true when we got our last raise. This wasn't true when Rita went from being a broke student at university to earning more money than she could spend. After travelling the world, Rodri realised that connection and stability were more important core needs for him.

Kaya, with a heart full of wisdom, embraces life's uncertainties. She relinquishes fixed expectations, finding comfort in the ever-changing nature of the world. With stoicism as her guiding light, she navigates obstacles with grace, transforming setbacks into stepping stones toward new habits. Kaya's daily meditation habit reminds her to see the beauty in unexpected outcomes, fostering a life filled with contentment.

Pause and reflect:

1. *If indulging in a 'bad habit' helps you reset your money habits, enjoy this little treat.*
2. *You can reinforce a positive financial routine with a reward to turn this behaviour into a lasting habit.*
3. *Remember to reward yourself within a minute of completing the behaviour for easy learning of the new habit.*
4. *Skip the celebration every once in a while to keep things fresh and exciting for your dopamine reward system.*
5. *Turn setbacks into stepping stones, finding contentment in the beauty of unexpected life outcomes.*

Epilogue

A journey beyond money.

According to yogic philosophy, we inherit emotional, mental and physical patterns referred to as: *samskaras*. Through repeating specific actions, samskaras are reinforced, leading to mindsets that are stored in our autonomic nervous system. Beyond money, mindsets can manifest in many different areas of our lives.

Consider this thought experiment:

In one universe, as a child you repeatedly observe your parents giving money to charitable causes. You pick up these traits of generosity and embody this mindset of abundance. For example, when someone asks for a little financial support at a crowded bus station, you immediately offer to pay for their bus fare. However, your mindset may have been different if you were not modelled with this behaviour. You may have been wired to be suspicious of strangers' requests or to avoid people altogether in public places. In a parallel universe, imagine growing up in a household with many siblings fighting for food. You experience fierce competition at the dinner table, feel jealous seeing the plate of your eldest sibling, and worry about not getting enough on your own plate. Later in life, you may unknowingly repeat this pattern when you go to a wedding reception and there is a buffet. Your mindset may be wired to pile as much food on your plate as possible, even when there is a lavish spread available.

In both universes, we may recognise how mindsets are all galaxies of samskaras. The ancient yogic practice brings our awareness to feelings as they occur in the mind, body, and consciousness. Similar ideas are interwoven into the stories of indigenous wisdom and other ancient practices. The philosophy behind maintaining a practice is to regularly shine the spotlight of attention on our own mindsets. It's about paying attention to why we feel what we feel, as we experience it. This is where our journey of rewiring begins.

A wise person also once said, "When the student is truly ready the teacher will disappear."

Bonus Quiz

Which money archetype am I? *Scan the QR code or find it here:*
www.behaviouralbydesign.com/money-mindsets

Notes

Introduction

1. Role of feelings. Damasio, A. (2019). *The strange order of things: Life, feeling, and the making of cultures.* Vintage.

We are wired for curiosity

1. Leslie, I. (2014). *Curious: The desire to know and why your future depends on it.* Basic Books.
2. Zellermayer, O. (1996). The pain of paying. *Carnegie Mellon University.*
3. Thomas, M., Desai, K. K., & Seenivasan, S. (2011). How credit card payments increase unhealthy food purchases: Visceral regulation of vices. *Journal of Consumer Research, 38(1),* 126-139.
4. Freakonomics. (2021, December 2). Everything you always wanted to know about money (but were afraid to ask). *Freakonomics Radio.* https://freakonomics.com/podcast/everything-you-always-wanted-to-know-about-money-but-were-afraid-to-ask/
5. Carlson, K., Kim, J., Lusardi, A., & Camerer, C. F. (2015). Bankruptcy rates among NFL players with short-lived income spikes. *American Economic Review, 105(5),* 381-84.

Frame your own money story

1. Maté, G., & Maté, D. (2022). *The myth of normal: Trauma, illness & healing in a toxic culture.* Random House.
2. Vedantam, S., & Mesler, B. (2021). *Useful delusions: The power and paradox of the self-deceiving brain.* WW Norton & Company.
3. CaRey, B. (2008). More expensive placebos bring more relief. *The New York Times.*
4. Tippett, K. (2020, July 1). Erik Vance — The drugs inside your head. *The On Being Project.* https://onbeing.org/prog rams/erik-vance-the-drugs-inside-your-head/
5. Sharif, M. A., & Shu, S. B. (2021). Nudging persistence after failure through emergency reserves. *Organizational Behavior and Human Decision Processes, 163,* 17-29.
6. Crum, A. J., & Langer, E. J. (2007). Mind-set matters: Exercise and the placebo effect. Psychological Science.

Nudge the system!

1. Madrian, B. C., & Shea, D. F. (2001). The power of suggestion: Inertia in 401(k) participation and savings behavior. *The Quarterly Journal of Economics, 116*(4), 1149-1187.
2. Vižintin, Ž., & Peksevim, S. (2021). How to increase your savings while spending. *Behavioral Scientist* https://behavio ralscientist.org/how-to-increase-your-savings-while-spen ding/
3. Milkman, K. L., Rogers, T., & Bazerman, M. H. (2010). I'll have the ice cream soon and the vegetables later: A study of online grocery purchases and order lead time. *Marketing*

Letters, 21(1), 17-35.

4. Krznaric, R. (2020). The good ancestor: How to think long term in a short-term world. Random House.

5. Reijula, S., & Hertwig, R. (2022). Self-nudging and the citizen choice architect. *Behavioural Public Policy, 6*(1), 119-149.

Seeing is believing

1. Ariely, D., & Kreisler, J. (2017). *Dollars and sense: Money mishaps and how to avoid them.* Boxtree.

2. Vedantam, S. (2022). You 2.0: The mind's eye. *Hidden Brain Media.* https://hiddenbrain.org/podcast/you-2-0-the-minds-eye/

3. Huberman, A. (2022). The science of setting & achieving goals. Huberman Lab. https://hubermanlab.com/the-science-of-setting-and-achieving-goals/

4. Benz, C., & Ptak, J. (2021). Hal Hershfield: People treat their future self as if it's another person. *Morningstar.* https://www.morningstar.com/articles/1058966/hal-hershfield-people-treat-their-future-self-as-if-its-another-person

5. Huberman, A. (2022, July 17). The science of setting & achieving goals. *Huberman Lab.* https://hubermanlab.com/the-science-of-setting-and-achieving-goals/

Setting goals with intention

1. Fishbach, A. (2022). *Get it done: Surprising lessons from the*

science of motivation. Macmillan.

2. Hershfield, H. E., Shu, S., & Benartzi, S. (2020). Temporal reframing and participation in a savings program: A field experiment. *Marketing Science, 39*(6), 1039-1051.

3. Allen, E. J., Dechow, P. M., Pope, D. G., & Wu, G. (2017). Reference-dependent preferences: Evidence from marathon runners. *Management Science, 63*(6), 1657-1672.

4. Milkman, K. (Host). (n.d.). The price of your vice: With guests Dan Ariely & Dean Karlan. *Choiceology.* https://www .schwab.com/learn/story/price-your-vice-with-guests-dan-ariely-dean-karlan

5. Akbas, M., Ariely, D., Robalino, D. A., & Weber, M. (2016). How to help poor informal workers to save a bit: Evidence from a field experiment in Kenya. *IZA Discussion Papers, 10024.*

Counting what matters

1. Housel, M. (2020). *The psychology of money: Timeless lessons on wealth, greed, and happiness.* Harriman House Limited.

2. Suits, B. (2014). *The grasshopper: Games, life and utopia.* Broadview Press.

3. Nguyen, C. T. (2021). The seductions of clarity. *Royal Institute of Philosophy Supplement, 89*, 227-255.

4. Fishbach, A. (2022). *Get it done: Surprising lessons from the science of motivation.* Macmillan.

5. Bleich, S. N., Barry, C. L., Gary-Webb, T. L., & Herring, B. J. (2014). Reducing sugar-sweetened beverage consumption by providing caloric information: How black adolescents

alter their purchases and whether the effects persist. *American Journal of Public Health, 104*(12), 2417-2424.

Context creates the habit

1. Sussman, A. B., & Alter, A. L. (2012). The exception is the rule: Underestimating and overspending on exceptional expenses. *Journal of Consumer Research, 39*(4), 800-814.
2. Christian, B., & Griffiths, T. (2016). Algorithms to live by: The computer science of human decisions. Macmillan.
3. Vedantam, S. (Host). (2022, August 2). Money 2.0: Why we bust our budgets. *Hidden Brain Podcast*. https://hiddenbrai n.org/podcast/money-2-0-why-we-bust-our-budgets/
4. The Pew Charitable Trusts. (2015). How do families cope with financial shocks? https://www.pewtrusts.org/en/r esearch-and-analysis/issue-briefs/2015/10/the-role-of-emergency-savings-in-family-financial-security-how-do-families
5. Wood, W. (2019). *Good habits, bad habits: The science of making positive changes that stick*. Pan Macmillan.
6. Milkman, K. L., & Beshears, J. (2009). Mental accounting and small windfalls: Evidence from an online grocer. *Journal of Economic Behavior & Organization, 71*(2), 384-394.

Consistency compounds

1. Wood, W. (2019). *Good habits, bad habits: The science of making positive changes that stick*. Pan Macmillan.
2. Housel, M. (2020). *The psychology of money: Timeless*

lessons on wealth, greed, and happiness. Harriman House Limited.

3. Clear, J. (2018). *Atomic habits: An easy & proven way to build good habits & break bad ones.* Penguin.
4. Duckworth, A. (2016). *Grit: The power of passion and perseverance* (Vol. 234). New York, NY: Scribner.
5. Duke, A. (2022). *Quit: The Power of Knowing When to Walk Away.* Penguin.
6. Lally, P., Van Jaarsveld, C. H., Potts, H. W., & Wardle, J. (2010). How are habits formed: Modelling habit formation in the real world. *European Journal of Social Psychology,* 40(6), 998-1009.

Reward the small wins

1. Milkman, K. (2021). *How to change: The science of getting from where you are to where you want to be.* Penguin.
2. Duhigg, C. (2013). *The power of habit: Why we do what we do in life and business.* Random House.
3. Sutherland, R. (2019). *Alchemy: The surprising power of ideas that don't make sense.* Random House.
4. Lembke, A. (2021). *Dopamine nation: Finding balance in the age of indulgence.* Penguin.
5. Ariely, D., & Kreisler, J. (2017). *Dollars and sense: Money mishaps and how to avoid them.* Boxtree.
6. Holiday, R. (2018). The Stoic Guide to Winning The War Of Reality vs. Expectations. *Daily Stoic.* https://dailystoic.com/reality-vs-expectations/

About the Author

Vishal is a serial experimenter, sourdough baker, *pranayama* (breathwork) practitioner, workshop facilitator, and founder of Behavioural by Design. He combines behavioural science with design and systems thinking to help teams with 'tools to think like a behavioural scientist'.

His role as Chief Behavioural Scientist involves: (1) Enabling banks and technology companies to create more behaviorally-informed products and services, (2) Building capability for the public sector in New Zealand to adopt behavioral science, and (3) Setting up experiments to help organisations test which strategies are most likely to change behaviours.

Vishal also chairs the New Zealand Behavioural Science Network, which brings together academia and industry to explore the application of behavioral science in socially relevant topics such as financial wellbeing, unconscious bias and sustainability.

P.S. I appreciate the time you've invested in reading my book. If you'd like to support my journey as an author, you can do so by leaving a review on Amazon or Goodreads.

You can connect with me on:
🌐 https://www.behaviouralbydesign.com

Made in the USA
Middletown, DE
03 January 2024

47161716R00073